Where One Voice Ends Another Begins

Where One Voice Ends

Another Begins

150 YEARS OF MINNESOTA POETRY

EDITED BY
Robert Hedin

MINNESOTA HISTORICAL SOCIETY PRESS

Permissions and additional copyright notices appear on pages 239–247.

www.mhspress.org

The Minnesota Historical Society Press is a member of the Association of American University Presses.

Manufactured in the United States of America

10 9 8 7 6 5 4 3 2 1

♾ The paper used in this publication meets the minimum requirements of the American National Standard for Information Sciences— Permanence for Printed Library Materials, ANSI Z39.48-1984.

International Standard Book Numbers
ISBN-13: 978-0-87351-584-9 (cloth)
ISBN-10: 0-87351-584-6 (cloth)

Library of Congress Cataloging-in-Publication Data

Where one voice ends another begins :
    150 years of Minnesota poetry / edited by Robert Hedin.
        p.   cm.
    Includes bibliographical references and index.
    ISBN-13: 978-0-87351-584-9 (cloth : alk. paper)
    ISBN-10: 0-87351-584-6 (cloth : alk. paper)
    1. American poetry—Minnesota.
    2. Minnesota—Poetry
    I. Hedin, Robert, 1949–
PS571.M6W48 2007
811'.00809776—dc22   2006035320

Where One Voice Ends Another Begins

To all the poets of Minnesota
who have enriched the literary heritage
of the state

1965–1985

1985–Present

Introduction

Compiled in celebration of Minnesota's sesquicentennial, *Where One Voice Ends Another Begins: 150 Years of Minnesota Poetry* gathers into a single volume one hundred and seventy-two selections from the state's rich poetic heritage. From the lyrics and oral traditions of the Dakota and the Ojibwe cultures to the premier modernist and contemporary poets of today, this anthology exemplifies the breadth of a vital and compelling tradition. Throughout the volume, poets evoke the lay and character of the land, depict tensions between farm and city life, and illuminate the geographic and cultural areas unique to Minnesota. Included are verses by poets of European heritage and of African American, Hispanic, Hmong, Japanese, and Chinese backgrounds that speak to the state's growing cultural diversity. Although subjects and styles vary throughout the volume, the poets' main concerns remain consistent: heritage and family life, loss and reclamation, the integrity of everyday events, and our proper place in the natural world with all its seasonal turnings and yearly migrations.

Behind each and every one of the poems is the undeniable conviction that poetry enriches the composition of life in Minnesota; that it is capable, perhaps more than any other human endeavor, of giving voice to the deepest yearnings of the spirit, and in doing so offers insights into who we are, where we have come from, our values and aspirations. Throughout the volume, poets break through the numbing, stultifying voice of our mass culture to successfully articulate a deeper circuitry that helps give life—and the life of the state—its necessary shape and substance. Ultimately, the poets in *Where One Voice Ends Another Begins* work toward the recovery of a fundamental ground, a place composed of shapes and contours, patterns and moments, that are common to us all, a shared property where we are able to regain a certain communality of spirit. In reading their work, a veil is lifted and we find ourselves startled and awakened, filled with a quickened sense of pleasure, of recognition, with something close to what we might call home.

· · · ·

Certainly, some of the finest pieces in *Where One Voice Ends Another Begins* are the many lyrics that rose out of the oral traditions of the Dakota and the Ojibwe cultures long before the arrival to the state of any white settlers. Handed down from one generation to another, they played an integral role in the social fabric of the community and acted as an important means of celebrating and preserving tribal culture and history. Translated by renowned musicologist Frances Densmore and the Reverend Alfred Longley Riggs, they constitute today a rich legacy that honors some of Minnesota's earliest inhabitants. Here, for example, is a portion from "My Love Has Departed," a spare and incisive Ojibwe love poem that captures, in a mere fourteen syllables, the profundity of human loss:

> A loon
> I thought it was
> But it was
> My love's
> Splashing oar.

Or this, titled "The Sioux Women Gather Up Their Wounded," a poignant lyric from the mid-eighteenth century, when the Dakota and the Ojibwe repeatedly did battle over valuable hunting-grounds in northern Minnesota:

> The Sioux women
>   pass to and fro wailing
>   as they gather up
>   their wounded men
> The voice of their weeping comes back
>   to us

Indeed, the earliest of verses by white settlers were vulgarizations of Dakota and Ojibwe myths. Published in the mid-nineteenth century, Samuel Pond's "An-pe-tu-sa-pa-win," Martha Pearson Smith's "Winona, A Legend of Maiden Rock," and Myron Coloney's long-winded *Manomin: A Rhythmical Romance of Minnesota* tended to cast the Indian in highly romanticized, melodramatic roles—an archetype that appealed to readers not only in the United States but in Europe, too, as seen in "Song of a Nadowessee Chief" by the German Romantic poet Friedrich von Schiller. Contemporary readers find in these poems little in the way of literary value, yet their popularity was longstanding, none more than Henry Wadsworth Longfellow's 1855 *Song of Hiawatha*, a poem that has been translated into at least twelve languages, including Latin, and was read and memorized by generations of American schoolchildren. Over a hundred and fifty years after its publication, it is arguably the best-known poem about the state.

By 1864, six years after Minnesota's entrance into the union, the state had produced enough poets for an anthology of its verse to be published: *Poets and Poetry of Minnesota*, edited by Mrs. W. J. Arnold. The book's twenty-two contributors were missionary teachers, Civil War heroes, politicians, and journalists for whom writing poetry was a secondary enterprise. They had been born and bred on the eastern seaboard and brought a New England literary sensibility to a region that was decidedly un–New England in almost every respect. It is at best a thoroughly unremarkable poetry, dominated by romantic idylls, sentimental elegies, overarching war exhortations, and unabashed anthems to progress, indebted to the works of Longfellow, John Greenleaf Whittier, and other hugely popular but ultimately minor poets of New England's "fireside" school. Composed in rhyming couplets and strict metronomic cadences, the poetry marched in lockstep in the rank and file of accepted poetic behavior and was designed to appeal to eastern readers—for this reason, there is no real palpable sense of the often bleak, spartan life of a pioneer, the dangers and mysteries of living in an untamed region, or the overall isolation and melancholy that abound on any thinly settled frontier.

Here is a portion of Mary Henderson Eastman's "The Seal of Minnesota," a poem about the white conquest of the state's Native American cultures, written in a language that plainly augurs Social Darwinism. Minnesota is presented in allegorical terms wherein the drama of Manifest Destiny is acted out, and, like many poets of her era, Eastman makes no attempt to imaginatively absorb the land or authentically portray the state's indigenous cultures:

> Give way, give way, young warrior,
> Our title would you seek?
> 'Tis "the rich against the poor,
> And the strong against the weak."
> We need the noble rivers,
> Thy prairies, green and wide,
> And thy dark and frowning forests
> That skirt the valley's side.

Minnesota poetry had lost virtually all its frontier connections by the late nineteenth century. Eastman's "dark and frowning forests" and "young warrior," for example, had been replaced by the "amber evening tints" and other irrepressibly romantic or fabulist images of Richard Burton's "Revery." At this time, the state had already turned from uncharted wilderness to plotted landscape, and was no longer a part of the "far west" but of the Midwest—a place of untold riches, burgeoning cities, and prairies transformed into what Arthur Upson called "golden floors" of wheat.

In the time of the world wars, it was the novel, not poetry, that was preeminent in Minnesota literature. Most of the major figures of this period—Kay Boyle, Beatrice Washburn Jones, Mary Ostenso, Meridel LeSueur, and F. Scott Fitzgerald—were prose writers who moonlighted as poets. Moreover, aside from Richard Eberhart and Joseph Warren Beach's work, Minnesota itself does not figure into the poetry at all. Depictions of farm and small town life, the state's growing urban centers, or the Depression years of the thirties: all these became the property of prose, of Lewis's *Main Street* and *Babbitt* and other naturalistic tomes fashionable to that era, not to mention LeSueur's essay "Women on the Breadlines," which detailed the plight of unemployed women in Minneapolis during the Depression. Notably, every writer of consequence fled the state at this time, usually never to return. As Richard Eberhart said, "When I was young, Minnesota was barren of cultural richness and I doubt that I would have matured or progressed as a poet if I had stayed there." In the case of Fitzgerald and Boyle, this meant the great tug of Paris and the Lost Generation writers of the twenties. Fitzgerald's Parisian years are well documented. Not so for Boyle, a largely forgotten Minnesota writer, though her years among the expatriate scene proved to be nothing short of a watershed. Still in her twenties and thousands of miles from her St. Paul roots, she became the literary confidante of the likes of Samuel Beckett and James Joyce, and published her first poems and stories in such influential Left Bank quarterlies as Eugene Jolas's *transition*. As for Jones, she entered the world of journalism and wrote for many high-powered dailies, includ-

ing the *New York Sun* and the *San Francisco Examiner,* while
LeSueur joined the radical, left-wing, political-literary circles
of New York and Hollywood.

Overall, the poetry from this period exhibits a greater
range and stylistic experimentation than the Minnesotan
verse of the nineteenth century. More importantly, the un-
abashed romanticism so dominant in the state's early lyrics
was replaced by the skepticism and self-consciousness we as-
sociate with the modernist sensibility. Nowhere is this
change better exemplified than in Boyle's "The Only Bird
That Sang," her grim, sobering portrait of the First World
War:

> The corporal died happy to have had
> A flower nourished by his nine red yards
> Of clogged intestines planted where he fell
> Others were put seven hundred at a time
> Under a truckload of small rock and gravel
> In a way that any group
> Could be disposed of without a loss to history
> Beyond beauty of line squandered and wiped out
> Tied still beneath gray wire wreaths with
> Petits anges au ciel volez volez pour nous
> Written in celluloid

It is doubtful whether Boyle could have written these lines if
she had stayed in Minnesota; it is more probable to assume
that her life in the rich literary salons of Paris, to say nothing
of her proximity to the great killing fields of the French front,
account for their real impetus. Richard Eberhart, though, did
turn to the state repeatedly for inspiration once he left Min-
nesota for good after his mother's death in 1922. A major
figure in the generation of American poets that emerged be-
tween the mid-1930s and the end of the Second World War,
Eberhart looked to his upbringing to ground many of his
most important poems, including "Orchard" and "The

Groundhog," the latter a staple in American high school text-books for decades.

. . . .

The years between World War II and the Vietnam War proved to be pivotal in the history of Minnesota poetry, wit-ness to a period of revolt that in many ways can be seen as a microcosm of the poetic revolution that was occurring na-tionally. This was the time of Lowell, of the Beats, of the Black Mountain poets—a time, in short, when American writers renounced modernism in favor of new aesthetics.

The state was now home to Carl Rakosi, Reed Whitte-more, Robert Penn Warren, John Berryman, Allen Tate, Robert Bly, James Wright, and Thomas McGrath. A remark-able generation of poets by any standard, it is rare to en-counter literary vitality of this order in a region so far removed from the traditional epicenter of New York. Un-doubtedly, a generous share of this vitality can be attributed to the willingness of several of these writers to break with the prevailing spirit of New Criticism. A postwar movement led by southern agrarian poet John Crowe Ransom, New Criti-cism believed that a poem could be studied as an isolated whole, separate from historical or psychological influences; the most vocal theoreticians of the movement, like Ransom and Tate, urged poets to treat contemporary themes and pre-occupations with conventional rhyme and meter. By no longer adhering to this attitude, a cadre of poets based in the state—Berryman, McGrath, Bly, and Wright—fundamentally altered the course of Minnesota poetry by jumpstarting it out of the formalism of previous eras and wedding it to contem-porary energies and innovations.

Warren and Tate resided in Minnesota for relatively lengthy periods of time—Warren from 1942–1951 and Tate from 1951–1968—but neither incorporated the state into their work in any significant fashion, choosing for the most part southern locales and subjects. Berryman, though, had strong ties to Minnesota. He came to the University in 1955, brought here largely through the influence of Tate, his old teacher at Columbia. Also, Berryman's father had been a native Minnesotan—though he committed suicide in 1925, when the poet was eleven years old. As a member of the University's department of humanities—where he shared an office for a time with Saul Bellow—Berryman developed a personalized, idiosyncratic voice marked by abrupt rhythmical and tonal shifts, a voice that was also committed to exploring his own inner life and turbulence. All of these traits ran contrary to the doctrine of the New Critics, and Berryman's use of them made way for an unusually prolific period: the eight years between 1956 and 1964, when he published *Homage to Mistress Bradstreet, Berryman's Sonnets,* and *77 Dream Songs,* three books concerned with what Berryman labeled "the epistemology of loss."

Thomas McGrath, too, broke with the dominant period style of the 1950s and sought out what he called "an internal keeping of form" while completing the 3,500-line opening sequence of *Letter to an Imaginary Friend.* Published in 1962, this overlooked poem is semiautobiographical in nature and steeped in Midwestern images reflective of McGrath's North Dakota roots.

In retrospect, no figure seems more influential to contemporary Minnesota poetry than Madison, Minnesota, native Robert Bly. In his poems and translations, as well as in the pages of his iconoclastic journal and press called *The Fifties* (later known successively as *The Sixties* and *The Seventies*), Bly advanced a verse freer even than Berryman's—one that contained juxtapositions and imaginative leaps of image and phrase designed to reflect the contours of the unconscious. Here, for example, are the first and last stanzas of "Driving Toward the Lac Qui Parle River," which begins in an unassuming and declarative voice, the author's shorthand registering an easily recognizable Minnesotan scene:

I am driving; it is dusk; Minnesota.
The stubble field catches the last growth of sun.
The soybeans are breathing on all sides.
Old men are sitting before their houses on car seats
In the small towns. I am happy,
The moon rising above the turkey sheds

. . . .

Nearly to Milan, suddenly a small bridge,
And water kneeling in the moonlight.
In small towns the houses are built right on the ground;
The lamplight falls on all fours in the grass.
When I reach the river, the full moon covers it;
A few people are talking low in a boat.

Employing a hint of the surreal—"lamplight falls on all fours
in the grass"—as well as archetypal images of light, bridge, and
water, Bly's poem deftly appropriates imagery of the objective
world to portray the driver's interior state. The moon has
reached its zenith, just as the narrator arrives at his own
fullest point—a highly distilled state of solitude, all rendered
through the usage of casual, everyday, indeed discernibly
Midwestern rhythms.

Bly's work proved decisive in helping Wright liberate him-
self from his earliest formalist influences, poets like Frost,
Robinson, and Hardy. Wright's 1963 book, *The Branch Will Not
Break,* published one year after Bly's debut volume, *Silence in the
Snowy Fields,* contains some of his most significant lyrics, in-
cluding "Lying in a Hammock at William Duffy's Farm in
Pine Island, Minnesota" and "A Blessing," two poems that
have earned a permanent place in the twentieth-century
canon. Above all, Bly and Wright's poems bore the indelible
mark of Minnesota, making the land and their new aesthetic
inseparable and teaching an entire generation of readers that
one could write about the state in a way that was not stale and
anachronistic—that Minnesota was capable of sustaining a vi-
able poetry.

If a true, identifiable voice—a voice that looked upon itself as self-consciously "Minnesotan"—showed signs of emerging in these decades, it was the twenty years from 1965 to 1985 that it achieved maturity. Indeed, no other period of Minnesotan history has inspired so much verse. This was due in part to the influences of Bly, Wright, and McGrath, and partly due as well to other cultural forces and developments. More colleges welcomed poets to their campuses, the state's poetry-in-the-schools program was initiated, such institutions as the Loft Literary Center opened their doors, and a number of new literary journals appeared, among them *Dacotah Territory, Great River Review, Moons and Lion Tailes, The North Stone Review,* and *Steelhead.* The state also became the home of several independent publishing houses—Graywolf Press, Holy Cow! Press, Milkweed Editions, New Rivers Press, and Nodin Press, for example—whose stables of writers included many Minnesotans. In addition, the National Endowment for the Arts, the Minnesota State Arts Board, and many private agencies such as the Bush and the McKnight foundations helped create a magnanimous climate of financial support for poets and publishers through grants and fellowships. Indeed, it was a heady time for poetry in Minnesota, and it took place on several fronts at once, involving poets, publishers, book distributors, independent bookstores, and an expanding, broad base of readers—all components necessary for a poetry community to thrive. Moreover, it was not imported from the outside, nor was it based entirely in the metropolitan areas of the Twin Cities. Instead, it occurred all over the state, in urban and rural areas alike.

For many poets during this time—John Calvin Rezmerski, Mark Vinz, Louis Jenkins, and Tom Hennen, for example—place, that deeply felt sense of locale, became paramount. They turned increasingly to the landscape and towns around them, and populated their poems with recognizable names and places—Willmar, Minneota, Owatonna, Long Prairie, Hinckley—producing a poetry that achieved an unprecedented intimacy with the state. For others, heritage became as important as place. They turned to their ancestral roots for inspiration and sustenance, a trend that would allow for the proliferation of multicultural voices in ensuing decades. In "Swedish Lesson," for example, Barton Sutter writes:

> I swear by my grandmother's face
> And steer to the north, northeast.
> I stammer and repeat my faith
> In the dead, their hope, their anguish,
> Buried alive in this, their language.

These years also saw the emergence of a host of young women poets, including Patricia Hampl, Jill Breckenridge, Margaret Hasse, Deborah Keenan, and others, many of whom explored their roles as women, as lovers, as daughters, and as mothers. At the same time, there appeared a small but important number of poets of color—Etheridge Knight, Marilyn Nelson, David Mura, and Louise Erdrich, for example. Subsequently, beginning in the mid-1980s, a growing body of verse emerged that dealt largely with experiences of later immigrants. Like earlier poets of Scandinavian or German extraction, many young, accomplished writers of African American, Native American, Hispanic, Hmong, Korean, and Chinese heritage began to delve into their ethnic identities and the tensions of being American with roots in other cultures.

Unlike immigrants of the nineteenth century, however, they confront not a wilderness but a contemporary Minnesota society they seem to have no hope of transforming. Alienated and disenfranchised, they find themselves caught in a kind of no-man's-land between their old cultures and a society in which they are often ignored, patronized, maligned, or worse. There is Wang Ping, for instance, whose "I Curse Because" and "Mixed Blood" are haunted by the utopian visions of America on the one hand and the crushing disillusionments of reality on the other. Or Mayli Vang and Mai Neng Moua, whose poems speak of gender and ethnic oppression—the suffocating "patriarchal rituals" of their Hmong community and those of a mainstream Minnesota culture that denies them the possibility of any kind of meaningful assimilation. Driven by the need to bring coherence to personal and collective experience, they turn back to their ethnic roots and speak of the nurturing influence of intergenerational relationships; for them, the dead and the living, the past and the present, are forever linked. As contemporary Ojibwe poet Denise Sweet writes in "Constellations":

> These are the new stories,
> our response
> to the sorrow
> of light arriving
> and dying
> the stellar maps of
> story and myth
> where writers find
> their way back
> to beginnings

Where One Voice Ends Another Begins concludes with "A Clerk's Tale," Spencer Reece's ironic nod to Chaucer's *Canterbury Tales*. Set in a deserted parking lot, Reece and his coworker pause on their pilgrimage into the night to watch the moon rise over one of the state's contemporary icons, the Mall of America, emblematic of the great change the state has undergone since its wilderness beginnings:

> This is how our day always ends.
> Sometimes snow falls like rice.
> See us take our dimly lit exits,
> disappearing into the cities of Minneapolis and St. Paul;
> Minneapolis is sleek and St. Paul,
> named after the man who had to be shown,
> is smaller, older, and somewhat withdrawn.

Behind us, the moon pauses over the vast egg-like dome
  of the mall.
See us loosening our ties among you.
We are alone.
There is no longer any need to express ourselves.

. . . .

In many ways, this anthology is a kind of inventory, a way
of taking stock at an important juncture in the state's history.
The book is divided into five sections, with each section rep-
resenting a major period of development in the history of
Minnesota poetry; as in any anthology, oversights and omis-
sions are bound to occur, and readers should bear in mind
that the book highlights only a sampling of the vast amount
of poetry written in Minnesota.

The criteria used to determine whether a poem was in-
cluded in the volume were simple. First, it had to be *good,* pos-
sessing a startling conviction of sound and voice; second, its
author had either to be native Minnesotan or to have spent a
significant amount of time in the state—enough time, that is,
for the area to markedly inform his or her sensibility. One-
fourth or so of these authors were born in Minnesota; the rest
adopted it as their home. In many cases, the number of years
certain authors spent thinking and writing about the state ex-
ceeded the time of their residency here. James Wright, for
instance: a native of Ohio who taught at the University of
Minnesota and Macalester College between 1957 and 1965,
Wright published many of his best poems about Minnesota—
works like "The Minneapolis Poem"—*after* he left the Twin
Cities. Regardless of the details and nuances of their biogra-
phies, every contributor has enriched the state's literary tra-
dition in obvious and considerable ways, and all comprise a
poetic community that has been in continual flux since the
mid-nineteenth century, one that has repeatedly renewed and
redefined itself with fresh styles and perspectives. In one

fashion or another, the poems in *Where One Voice Ends Another Begins* can all be accurately called Minnesotan, a label that should not in any way suggest their limitations or paucity of vision, or deny their great reach and immediacy. Throughout the book, poets summon the supreme and ongoing human desire to make of life something meaningful, and in doing so they echo a set of questions as ancient and enduring as literature itself. Homer tells us that upon Odysseus's return to Ithaca, the hero—not yet aware that this was his homeland—looked out and asked:

Tell me this and tell me truly, so that I may know.
What land is this? What community? What people live here?

ROBERT HEDIN
Red Wing, Minnesota
2007

Where One Voice Ends Another Begins

Beginnings–1914

◆   ◆   ◆   ◆   ◆   ◆   ◆

Song-Poems of the Dakota (Sioux)

Translated by Frances Densmore and Alfred Longley Riggs

An American pioneer in the field of ethnomusicology, Frances Densmore (1867–1957) was born in Red Wing and educated at the Oberlin Conservatory of Music. Over her forty-year career, she made more than 2,500 sound recordings of Native American music, published 22 books, and wrote more than 200 articles. Her chief works include Chippewa Music, Chippewa Music II, *and the monumental study,* Teton Sioux Music. *The Smithsonian–Densmore Collection forms a major part of the Archives of American Folk Songs in the Library of Congress. Densmore's translations are from her 1917 publication,* Poems from Sioux and Chippewa Songs, *and were done with the assistance of Robert Higheagle.*

Missionary and translator Alfred Longley Riggs (1837–1916) was born at the Lac Qui Parle Mission and was a leading authority on the Dakota language. Educated at Knox College and the Theological Seminary in Chicago, he established the Congregational Mission at the Santee Agency to the Sioux in Nebraska in 1870 and later founded the Santee Normal Training School, a boarding school in which instruction was conducted in the Dakota language.

Song at Sunrise

The rising sun in the east shining,
Speaketh to us in his glorious splendor,
"I am the sun; see me in my rising.
Lo, I am the sun,
Behold with blinded eyes,
I am the sun!"

Song of a Warrior

O, my friends, as I stand
Here before you all assembled,

I hear you sing of the lands where the warriors travel.
O, my friends, the many lands that you fear,
In them all without fear I have walked.
O, my friends, even now
I can see the distant mountains
Where the snows never melt in the summer time.
O, my friends, I have walked without fear in those lands,
For there I sought the black face-paint.

To the west and the north
Lies the country of the enemy.
In all those lands I have walked without fear of harm.
O, my friends, in them all I have won the right to wear
The warrior's badge of victory.

Old Sioux Love Song

Go thou with the warriors,
Go thou forth to war;
Go thou forth with the warriors,
When I hear the Crier shout your name with the victors,
Then, ah then, I will marry you.

I will stay in the village,
I will sit with the women
All day making moccasins,
Listening always for the signal cry that the warriors come,
Then, ah then, I may marry you.

[F. D.]

Songs of War

I have cast in here a soul,
I have cast in here a soul,

I have cast in here a buffalo soul;
    I have cast in here a soul.
      . . . .
I make my way with my face covered,
I make my way with my face covered;
    The people are buffaloes;
I make my way with my face covered.
      . . . .
    Night now passes along,
    Night now passes along;
It passes along with a thunder bird;
    Night now passes along.
      . . . .
    Whose sacred road lies plainly,
    Whose sacred road lies plainly;
The sacred road of day lies plainly.
      . . . .
    Ojibwa, hurry along!
    Ojibwa, get out of the way!
We're coming there again.
      . . . .
    Terrifying all I journey,
    Terrifying all I journey;
By the *Toon-kan'* at the North,
    Terrifying all I journey.
      . . . .
    Something I've killed, and I lift up my voice,
    Something I've killed, and I lift up my voice;
The northern buffalo I've killed, and I lift up my voice;
    Something I've killed, and I lift up my voice.

                       [A. L. R.]

. . . .

Song-Poems of the Ojibwe (Anishinaabe/Chippewa)

Translated by Frances Densmore

"I heard an Indian drum when I was very, very young," Frances Densmore wrote, "and I have followed it across the continent." In 1907, she traveled to the northern part of Minnesota to record and transcribe the songs of the Ojibwe. The following were translated by Densmore with the assistance of Mary Warren English and the Reverend C. H. Beaulieu.

The Sioux Women Gather Up Their Wounded

The Sioux women
        pass to and fro wailing
        as they gather up
        their wounded men.
The voice of their weeping comes back
        to us.

Song Sung Over a Dying Person

You are a spirit,
I am making you a spirit,
In the place where I sit
I am making you a spirit.

Song of an Ambitious Mother

This I have come to ask you,
This I have come to ask you—
O, let your daughter
Marry my son, the hunter,
And he'll give your daughter
My big brass kettle.

Love Song

All my heart is lonely,
All my heart is full of sorrow.
My lover, my lover is departed.

Dark the sky at evening,
Sad the bird-notes in the dawning.
My lover, my lover is departed.

He was all my sunshine,
His the beauty and the gladness.
Return, return, gladness and joy.

In Her Canoe

In her canoe I see her,
Maiden of my delighted eyes.
I see in the rippling of the water
The trailing light slipped from her paddle blade.
A signal sent to me.
Ah, maiden of my desire,
Give me a place in thy canoe;
Give me the paddle blade,
And you shall steer us away
Wherever you would go!

My Love Has Departed

1.
A loon
I thought it was
But it was
My love's
Splashing oar.

2.
To Sault Ste. Marie
He has departed
My love
Has gone on before me
Never again
Can I see him.

. . . .

MARY HENDERSON EASTMAN
(1818–1887)

Mary Henderson Eastman came to Minnesota in the 1840s with her hus-
band, artist Seth Eastman, and settled at Fort Snelling. She was the author
of several books, including Aunt Phyllis's Cabin, *a reply to Harriet*
Beecher Stowe's Uncle Tom's Cabin, *and* Dacotah; or, Life and
Legends of the Sioux Around Fort Snelling, *an influence on*
Henry Wadsworth Longfellow's famous 1855 poem, Song of Hiawatha.

The Seal of Minnesota

The design is, the Indian retreating as civilization advance[s]—The white
man, the plough, axe, powder horn and rifle, in the foreground. St. Anthony's
Falls in the distance.

Give way, give way, young warrior,
Thou and thy steed give way—
Rest not, though lingers on the hills
The red sun's parting ray.
The rocky bluff and prairie land,
The white man claims them now,
The symbols of his course are here,
The rifle, axe, and plough.

Give way, give way, young warrior,
Our title would you seek?

'Tis "the rich against the poor,
And the strong against the weak."
We need the noble rivers,
Thy prairies, green and wide,
And thy dark and frowning forests
That skirt the valley's side.

The Redman's course is onward—
Nor stayed his footsteps be,
Till by his rugged hunting ground
Beats the relentless sea!
We claim his noble heritage,
And Minnesota's land
Must pass with all its untold wealth
To the white man's grasping hand.

Give way,—I know a thousand ties
Most lovingly must cling,
I know a gush of sorrow deep
Such memories must bring;
Thou and thy noble race from earth
Must soon be passed away,
As echoes die upon the hills,
Or darkness follows day.

.   .   .   .

James H. Baker
(1829–1913)

James H. Baker was born in Monroe, Ohio, and graduated from Ohio Wesleyan University. In 1857, he ventured to Minnesota and settled on a farm near Mankato. The following year he was elected secretary of state. From 1862 to 1863, he fought under General Henry H. Sibley in campaigns against the Dakota and later was appointed provost-marshal of the Department of Missouri, a position he held until the close of the Civil War. In 1865, he re-

turned to Minnesota, where he held various state offices, including railroad commissioner and surveyor general of the state of Minnesota.

A Sea Song

Down, deep in the depths
  Of the fathomless sea,
Lie ingots of wealth
  We never shall see;
So, down in the depths
  Of the measureless heart,
Lies a richness of love
  Unfathomed by art.

With the bright blue waves
  Caressing our keel,
Of the wealth of the ocean
  How little we feel;
Of the tide of immortals
  We meet and we part,
How little we know
  Of the depths of the heart.

The caves of the ocean
  Have each in their cell
The soft-sighing music
  Of a rose-tinted shell;
So love is the music
  That deep in the breast,
Gives beauty to being,
  And sweetness to rest.

Take the bright shell
  From its home on the lea,
And wherever it goes

It will sing of the sea;
So take the fond heart
   From its home and its hearth,
It will sing of the loved
   To the ends of the earth.

. . . .

IGNATIUS DONNELLY
(1831–1901)

Reformer, public official, and author, Ignatius Donnelly was born and raised in Philadelphia, Pennsylvania, and came to Minnesota in 1856. On the banks of the Mississippi near St. Paul, he founded the town of Nininger in the hopes of establishing a great Western metropolis. From 1859 to 1862, he served as Lieutenant Governor of Minnesota, and later was elected to both the House of Representatives and the state senate. One of Minnesota's great orators, he played a leading role in various reform movements and helped found the Populist Party. He was the author of Atlantis: The Antediluvian World, Ragnarok: The Age of Fire and Gravel, Caesar's Column, *and other books that reached a worldwide audience.*

A Description

Not the great, gaudy presence and rude charms,
That kept, of old, contending camps in arms—
But delicate in figure, face and mind,
Formed to enchant and civilize mankind;
All the fine attributes of soul to move,
And fill the measure of fastidious love.
Here learning's light grows brilliant in dark eyes;
Here beauty's lips teach wisdom to the wise;
Here antique truths fall freshened from the tongue

Of one whose life is pure, whose heart is young.
As when the Chinese shade's raised figures stand,
Wrought almost perfect by the artist's hand,
And yet uneven, callous, cold and dull
Till the bright taper fills them, clear and full:
So woman's face, moulded by skill divine,
Graced with angelic beauty in each line,
But meaningless and soulless, meets the sight
Till intellect comes fresh'ning it with light;
And then, ah! then, each feature teems with grace,
Mind, softened mind, looks saint-like from the face;
In each sweet, dimpled smile the light lies caught,
And in the deep eyes dwell whole worlds of thought.

.   .   .   .

RICHARD BURTON
(1861–1940)

Richard Burton was born in Hartford, Connecticut, and educated at Trinity College, John Hopkins University, and the University of Southern California. He came to the University of Minnesota in 1898 and taught in the department of English for nearly a quarter of a century. He was the author of over twenty volumes of poetry, essays, literary biographies, and criticisms, including Poems of Earth's Meaning, Dumb in June, *and* Collected Poems.

Revery

EVENING

Dim grows the wood; the amber evening tints
    Merge into opal skies and stars just seen;
Down vistas gloomed and winding there are hints
    Of elves and gnomes along the mosses green.

MIDNIGHT

A holy song the thrush has distant-sung;
    The treetops murmur like some dreaming sea;
Hark! far away a silvern bell has rung
    Twelve strokes, slow tolled, that faint and fade from me.

MORNING

A shaft of gold upon my upturned face
    As fleeting and as shy as any fawn;
Sweet odors, stirring winds and forms of grace;
    Now tell me, is this heaven, or is it dawn?

The Lark

I stood knee-deep within a field of grain,
And felt a sudden flash of facile wings
That off the ground rose straight into the blue.
And looking, saw it was the lark, a wight
In all my days I had not glimpsed at home,
And now must find beyond the foam-white seas
For the first time. This child of ecstasy
Shook down roulades of song, and clove the air
Up, up and ever up toward very heaven,
A speck of buoyant life against the sky,
And bird-kind's one embodiment of soul
In God-aspiring flight. Across my mind
Rushed Shakespeare's hymn and Shelley's heavenly lay,
Wherein this bird, etherealized, becomes
More beautiful, and less of mortal mold;
Until half-dazed I stood, nor hardly knew
Whether I heard the descant of the lark,
Or those dear singers of the human race
Make subtle music for my brooding ear.

.   .   .   .

ARTHUR UPSON
(1877–1908)

Arthur Upson was born in Camden, New York, and moved with his family to St. Paul in 1894. A prominent figure in the Minnesota literary scene at the turn of the century, Upson graduated from the University of Minnesota, where in 1906 he was appointed to a position in the department of English. Despite a life of little money and repeated illnesses, he authored five books of poetry—At the Sign of the Harp, West Wind Songs, The City, Tides of Spring, *and* Octaves Written in an Oxford Garden— *as well as several verse plays. On August 14, 1908, at the age of thirty-one, he drowned while on vacation at Lake Bemidji.* The Collected Poems of Arthur Upson, *a two-volume set edited by his dear friend and mentor Richard Burton, was published in 1909.*

From the Valley of the Wheat

I sing to the trample of feet on golden floors—
    A continent's court whose dust is drifting gold;
I chant with the voice of the flood that over it pours
    Five hundred leagues at a lapse to the huge Gulf's hold.

I sing to the yielding of bolts of mountain doors,
    To the echoes of iron that beat their measures bold,
While, east and west, to the strain of bursting stores,
    Five hundred leagues asunder, the gates unfold.

Where the blind, quick seed of life for a thousand shores
    Is blest by the harrow that sinks in the silent mold,
I sing to the tremble of steel where the trestle roars,
    I chant to the throbbing of ships on seas untold!

Among the Pines

(Lake Bemidji, August 13, 1908)

The earnest pines are of the sober North.
　　Cold twilights find them sombre as themselves,
　　And the gold sun that down the red West delves
Like broken-lancéd knights doth set them forth.

There is among them only Autumn cheer,
　　A mournful sweetness—yet they do not change,
　　And their laced limbs are never bare and strange
Under the swift reprisals of the year.

If constancy brings melancholy joy,
　　This then is why these forests reach my heart
　　With their deep changeless tones, why tears do start
To-night when I behold their brave deploy.

Their constancy brings feelings linked to those
The soul brought here, and keeps beyond life's close.

.　.　.　.

HENRY ADAMS BELLOWS
(1885–1939)

A native of Maine, Henry Adams Bellows was educated at Harvard and later taught there in the department of English. In 1910, he moved to Minnesota to teach rhetoric at the University. After leaving his post in 1912, he held a variety of broadcasting positions in Minneapolis and also worked for the Minneapolis Daily News *and the Minnesota Orchestra. From 1912 to 1919, he served as managing editor of* The Bellman, *one of Minnesota's first successful literary journals. The author of one collection of poetry, Bellows is best known for his monumental translation of* The Poetic Edda, *a compilation of early Icelandic verse on cosmology, mythology, and the stories of Norse heroes that is considered a masterpiece of Northern European literature.*

West and East

A vast new land half wakened to the wonder
    Of mighty strength; great level plains that hold
Unmeasured wealth; and the prophetic thunder
    Of triumphs yet untold.

A land of eager hearts and kindly faces,
    Lit by the glory of a new-born day;
Where every eye seeks the far-distant places
    Of an untravelled way.

Oh generous land! Oh mighty inspiration
    That floods the morning of the world to be!
Thy people are the builders of a nation,
    Lofty, benignant, free.

Yet, at a trivial word, a star's clear gleaming,
    A bird's sweet song, a sunset fading fast,
There comes a longing for the homeland, dreaming
    Upon its sacred past.

A land of dear, remembered faces, moving
    Through happy days that had to have an end;
Each stream is a companion known and loving,
    And every hill a friend.

A longing to behold the mountains, rearing
    Their great, gaunt heads; and once again to be
Upon the barren, wind swept headland, hearing
    The surges of the sea.

1914–1945

◆   ◆   ◆   ◆   ◆

Joseph Warren Beach
(1880–1957)

Joseph Warren Beach was born in Gloversville, New York, and graduated from the University of Minnesota, where in 1907 he became a faculty member in the department of English. He was the author of numerous critical works, the novel Glass Mountain, *and several poetry collections, including* Sonnets of the Head and Heart, Beginning with Plato, *and* Involuntary Witness.

from *Minneapolis Skylines: 1915*

THE CHIMNEYS

Now the dusk settles over river and city,
Dim, rolling vapors rise to meet the crawling,
Heavy breath of the chimneys brown and murky,
And joining forces in the deepening twilight,
They make advance in one dark, ghostly tide.
Already it has filled the river-bottoms,
And steadily rises round the spindling legs
Of the airy bridges, till they are overwhelmed.
Now vanish gable, spire, and all that pictures
Our human life and labor along the skies.
The fog has drawn its smutty finger across
The clear gold of the fading sunset. Only,
As lone survivors of the submerged city,
Four slender shafts rise black upon the gold,
Piercing the smother: idle as in a dream,
Four clustered smokestacks. Having clean forgotten
Their daily toil, with what serene detachment
They lift their nostrils in the golden air,
As if they had no part nor interest
In the cloudy fortunes of the world below!

POWER

Moveless he stands against the iron railing,
With all the world about him in commotion.

The mighty water races on beneath him
To storm the falls. From the unnumbered chimneys
Flutters the smoke in long wind-shredded pennons.
The switching engines, blowing clouds of steam,
Tear back and forth, while over its granite arches
Thunders the night express, steady as fate,
With pomp of banners and proud illumination.
On every hand is power visible,
And yonder where the mills and powerhouses
Are lighting up their tier on tier of windows
Intenser it moves in spinning shaft and wheel,
Or lurks disguised in sleek and humming turbines.
Yet in that quiet figure by the railing,
Frail as a wisp between the sky and water,
Labors the sovereign force of all the planet.
Master of all the powers of earth and air,
He well may gaze upon his harnessed river
And stand unmoved amidst the hurly-burly.

BOHEMIAN FLATS
One side the river burrows deep beneath
The wooded cliffs with ragged stone outcroppings.
The other side it shuns the ancient banks
And so embraces in its curving elbow
A little flock of low-roofed huts that nestle
About the feet of the great straddling bridges.
How far below they lie, like some enchanted
Town in the weedy hollows of the ocean!
The cottonwoods that wave their lofty plumes
Above the ridgepole creep along the bottoms,
And even the wooden spire that herds the faithful
From end to end of the village, reaching upward,
Rests in the shadow of the railway trestles.
Those that speed past above by train or trolley
Are unaware of a world that lies beneath them.
And the glaring light of the lamps that swing on high
Falls dim and dreamlike on the sunken village,

Strained through fathoms of fog that lie above it.
No rumor comes to us aloft. They seem
Buried away beneath the care and fever
Of our insatiate struggle, as we fancy
Some sleepy village in a mountain valley
Ages and ages past, and far away.

. . . .

BEATRICE WASHBURN JONES
(1891–1984)

Beatrice Washburn Jones was born in Chicago, Illinois, raised in Minnesota, and educated at New England educational institutions and Les Marronniers in Paris, France. She worked as a reporter for a number of our nation's leading newspapers, including the Minneapolis Tribune, *the* New York Sun, *the* San Francisco Examiner, *and the* Miami Herald, *where she served as book editor. Her poetry, feature articles, book reviews, and translations appeared in hundreds of national publications.*

The Road to Asola

As we rode down to Asola
A thousand years ago,
The olive trees beside the way
Bent down their heads so low
To watch us as we passed along,
And, on the hills near by,
The almond flowers softly laid
Their cheeks against the sky.

We knew the road to Asola
Those centuries ago.
The glad acacias lightly danced

Along the fields to show
A golden pathway for our feet;
We wandered where it led.
The eucalyptus gravely bowed
Their crowns above our head.

Along the road to Asola,
We rode in years gone by.
We watched the drowsy mountains melt
Into the evening sky.
We saw the tired sun go down
And fall across our way,
While down the valleys sang the sea
Just as it does today.

The Transport

I watched your transport sail away for France
And tried to tell you then how brave you were,
How much I loved you, how the coming years
Were glorified; how all our little dreams
That we had built together sailed with you;
And of that winter day when we first met—
And how there was a new moon in the sky.
Do you remember when, like splintered ice
It lay upon the surface of the lake?
Oh how I loved you, and the wasted years
We might have spent together, but it still
Was something to have had, those happy years,
Something to hold, something to thank Him for,
Something most people die with never having known,
Something the war can never take away.
All this I would have told you but so much
Was left unsaid. We only talked of ships
And why the gulls could dip their wings so deep

And how the sky-line changes with the years,
And of the city, and be sure to write
And tell me everything you think of France,
And don't forget!—And then the whistle blew.

Now when they talk of war I only see
The harbor flashing in the sun, the dipping gulls,
The ragged edge of rope that tied the ship,
A little crack upon the painted rail
Where you last laid your hand.

.　.　.　.

F. Scott Fitzgerald
(1896–1940)

"It is what it is," F. Scott Fitzgerald wrote of poetry, "because an extraordinary genius paused at that point in history and touched it." The author of such American classics as This Side of Paradise, The Beautiful and Damned, The Great Gatsby, Tender Is the Night, *and* The Last Tycoon, *as well as of numerous short stories and essays, Fitzgerald was born in St. Paul, educated at Yale University, and led a short, tumultuous, and highly prolific literary life. Although not known as a poet, he wrote poetry all his life, mostly song lyrics, rhyming banter, and comedic doggerel.* Poems 1911–1940, *a posthumous collection, was published in 1981.*

We Leave To-night . . .

We leave to-night . . .
　　Silent, we filled the still, deserted street,
　　　A column of dim gray,
　　And ghosts rose startled at the muffled beat
　　　Along the moonless way;

The shadowy shipyards echoed to the feet
   That turned from night and day.

And so we linger on the windless decks,
   See on the spectre shore
Shades of a thousand days, poor gray-ribbed wrecks . . .
   Oh, shall we then deplore
Those futile years!
                   See how the sea is white!
The clouds have broken and the heavens burn
   To hollow highways, paved with gravelled light
The churning of the waves about the stern
   Rises to one voluminous nocturne,
                   We leave to-night.

.   .   .   .

KAY BOYLE
(1902–1993)

A native of St. Paul, Kay Boyle began her literary life in Paris during the 1920s, becoming friends with such writers as Samuel Beckett and James Joyce. From 1923 to 1941, she lived in Austria, England, and France, and from 1946 to 1953 she was a foreign correspondent for The New Yorker. *Upon her return to the United States, she taught for seventeen years at San Francisco State University. A recipient of numerous awards and honors for her writing, including two Guggenheim Fellowships, two O. Henry Awards, and the Before Columbus Foundation for her lifetime of work, she was a member of the National Institute of Arts and Letters and authored more than two dozen volumes of fiction, nonfiction, translations, and children's stories, as well as five volumes of poetry.*

The Only Bird That Sang

The church mice had been bombed out of Albert
The corporal under the gas ring
Said he would get out for good this time
If the roquefort didn't sit still on the plate
Instead of bruising its bottom green on the table.
For the French it was the way it ought to be
The roquefort but the corporal had a sore throat
And it had been raining all day

    They have planted a flower
    Under the rose trees at Albert
    Pneumonia cool as edelweiss
    Was the last thing blooming into a song for him
    Singing to him like a mama
    This century the war that came whistling
    The only bird that sang

After forty-eight hours of marriage with the elements
The corporal took out the roquefort
He had brought with him for company
It was winging in his pocket like a hummingbird
In Amiens he felt it out saying soit sage to it
In Albert he saw the gangrene on it was eating closer
And closer to the bone

    Spring came
    Without pulpit flowers
    Or boiling tubs of sassafras
    A long time
    Since spring had come in a new way
    The cannons bucked like goats
    Along the edge of it
    The veins broke wide and flowered
    The corporal at Albert
    Fell into decay

In response to the bird's clarion
There came the highest qualities of gentlemen
The girls (all ladies) nursing their way through it
The towns were proud the trains the sky the liners
Staterooms wharves the skyline proud
The army proud to wear them strong as hyacinths
The surgeons were happy and proud
The wings of airplanes and proud the sheets
The pillows bedpans congressmen the subways proud
The president the frigidaire turned proud
We are proud of our girls who are over there.

      Oh, Leda, how did the swan fly in hospitals
      How from the rushes did its wings lift
      The iron mirror of the lake
      Churned to a wheel from indolence to anger
      The small black budding spring
      Pressed close between the breasts

The corporal died happy to have had
A flower nourished by his nine red yards
Of clogged intestines planted where he fell
Others were put seven hundred at a time
Under a truckload of small rock and gravel
In the way that any group
Could be disposed of without a loss to history
Beyond beauty of line squandered and wiped out
Tied still beneath gray wire wreaths with
Petits anges au ciel volez volez pour nous
Written in celluloid

      I remember them
      With Christmas trees
      With lollypops
      Eating their soup quietly
      Out of the sides of their spoons

They made life a meal of
Young chop suey fresh roots and tendrils
Of peaches burning
And of lemon ice

The corporal died knowing that if Debs
Had been president there'd be a German general
In every maiden lady's bed
Contented to masturbate the lady mules
In spare time
Talking of war not as it was to him
A burden which in honor he could not put down

There will be more sons
More husbands fathers
To breed for another springtime
To stamp for another season for hallelujah
(Not the pruning and the sobbing of ringdoves
In the willows soft with repining)
Now we are stricken with peace
We are stricken with peace
We are stricken

O *This Is Not Spring*

O this is not spring but in me
there is a murmuring of new things
This is the time of a dark winter in the heart
but in me are green traitors

The dead lie apart with their throats laid full with sorrow
And the blood of the living moves slow in the cold
There is no one
To play the street like a flute with me
For a return on the old footsteps

They say write to me how the snow falls this winter
And if the horse sets out well on the road
And I answer
This year the blood cannot lie quiet
And the sun goes swift, swift through the hair

.   .   .   .

SISTER ALICE GUSTAVA (MARIS STELLA) SMITH
(1899–1987)

*A native of Alton, Iowa, Sister Alice Gustava (Maris Stella) Smith received
her early education at the Kirkwood School and the Drake Conservatory of
Music in Des Moines. In 1920, she entered the Sisters of St. Joseph of Caron-
delet in St. Paul and attended the College of St. Catherine and later Oxford
University. In 1929, she joined the faculty of St. Catherine's, where she
taught music, literature, and creative writing. Her volumes of poetry include*
Here Only A Dove, Frost for St. Brigid, *and* Collected Poems.
*"Autumn Paray-le-Monial" refers to the city in central France, second only
to Lourdes as a religious pilgrimage site.*

Autumn Paray-le-Monial

I can remember how in that old town
the yellow leaves of the plane tree fell in showers,
great yellow plane leaves, drifting, drifting down,
all afternoon, into the dusky hours.
All afternoon, filling the mellow air,
no sound of voice, no hum of bee or bird;
only the plane leaves rustling, rustling. There
was no other sound but rustling to be heard.
There was no other sound. The silver fog in clouds
covered the meadows, crept up all the trees,

the road was lined with ghosts in silver shrouds—
no sight or sound, save when a little breeze
startled the yellow plane leaves from the height,
rustling, rustling through the foggy night.

Riddles

Out of this tangle of threads to find the thread
that will untangle the threads. Out of the maze
to find the amazing path and so be led
back to the beginning by incredible ways.
Out of confusion of keys to find the key
that fits each keyhole, unlocks every lock.
Among a multitude of suns to see
only the sun. To find the moveless rock
under the shifting stones, under the sand,
the rock no shifting sands can ever shake,
nor great wind crying out over a shaken land,
nor lightning blast, nor breaking water break.
To find in multiplicity but one
end, beginning, thread, path, key, rock, sun. . . .

. . . .

MARTHA OSTENSO
(1900–1963)

Martha Ostenso was born in Bergen, Norway, and immigrated to the United States with her family at the age of two. She was educated in the rural schools of Minnesota and South Dakota, and later attended the University of Manitoba in Winnipeg. Upon returning to the United States in 1921, she attended Columbia University and later worked as a writer for the Bureau of Charities in Brooklyn, before embarking on a career as a freelance writer. A long-time resident of St. Louis Park, she was the author of one volume of poetry, A

Far Land, *and numerous novels, including* Wild Geese, The Dark
Dawn, *and* The Waters Under the Earth.

Brushwood

If there be anything of God left in the world
It must be here he walks on full-moon nights.

By day there's not a sorry crow would tilt:
A rusty tail upon the broken fence
That now and then leans on the empty air
As if it still kept something in or out.
The sun will show you traces of the flame
That lost seasons since came down the wind
And ate the very souls out of the trees;
Stunted, youngish poplars, overleafed
To hide the truth about their inner selves,
And willows blotched and matted at the roots—
Prayer rugs, you'll say, they're kneeling on.
The grass—it isn't grass. The earth is here
A wasted crone who wears a wig of thatch.
By day the lowest cloud will shun this place.
But when the light has gone, some secret gate
Swings open with the sound of coming wings,
Forgotten dreams steal in and wake the wood—
Perhaps a long gone lover comes and walks
With it and sings a tender little song.
It is a world of dew—and shadow—light,
And darkling shoals of silence where they blend.
And here the million little poplar discs
Quiver like a single misty gem
Fallen from some burdened star to earth.
You may pause and be a giant gnome
In a fairy forest where the dew
Is white wine cupped in shallow chrysoprase.
You may listen farther than the moon

To the enchanted converse of the stars.
You may listen just within the ring
Of glow-worm light you're standing in and hear
A wakeful little cricket's afterthought.
Or you may listen nearer till the mist
Encloses but the beating of your heart.

If there be anything of God abroad the earth,
I think he listens here when there's a moon.

.   .   .   .

MERIDEL LeSUEUR
(1900–1996)

*Meridel LeSueur was born in Murray, Iowa, and attended school in the
Twin Cities. After graduating from the American Academy of Dramatic
Art in New York City, she ventured to Hollywood, where she worked as a
stunt artist. She later served on the staff of the* New Masses *and wrote for*
The American Mercury, The Partisan Review, The Nation,
and Scribner's Magazine. *Acclaimed as a major writer in the thirties,
she was blacklisted during the McCarthy era for her left-wing politics.
Among her many published works are* North Star Country, Corn Vil-
lage, Rites of Ancient Ripening, Ripening: Selected Work
1927–1980, *and* Harvest Songs, *for which she received an American
Book Award.*

Spring Out of Jerusalem

The olive branch has budded
And secret Gethsemane is misted in creation.
Out of Golgotha a flower.
From the anointment of the Magdalene
Have come red flowers and crocuses.

Come forth!
The stone has rolled away and the tomb is empty.
Come forth!
The fruit, the body, and the wine.
Come forth!
The cross has budded and the thorn ends
Have blossomed!
Buds break on the thorns of ancient crucifixion.
Blood dripping from the nimbus of divinity
Has burst open the thorn ends in buds.
Buds swell and break from the wood of the cross.
The staff of the executioner has budded,
The seal of the tomb has burst asunder.
Trumpet has been raised to invisible lips and sounded
In the sap.
Come forth! Come forth!
Out of the damp tomb.
Out of the rock-sealed caves
Come forth!

Surround of Rainbows

The doorway to my home is made of light
Restore and return the body
                    call it home.
Walk toward me now
Let all tongues ring
Quicken the thighs and breast
                    the brain clangs
Strikes the horizon bell
                    all quickens
All things open in the She Rain.
Growing happily
            We return to our herds
                to our hogans
                    to jingling tassels

belling of sheep.
Someone is drumming
beating the sky.
Corn reaches up
She Rain reaches down
Juices spring out of dry thorns
Forgotten bones flesh with forgotten men.
I entered the living water
It fell upon my starving bones.
Blue corn tied with white lightning
and the rains come
upon me too.
Restore us all
The land the man the woman child beast
Insect   all creatures beasts and herbs
Restore us here
Tie us with the blue bean, the great squash
Surround of rainbows
Listen
The rain comes upon us
Restore us.

. . . .

RICHARD EBERHART
(1904–2005)

Richard Eberhart was born in Austin and educated at the University of Minnesota, Dartmouth College, and Cambridge. Upon graduation, he worked briefly as an advertising copywriter and as a deckhand on a tramp steamer. He served as a tutor to the son of King Prajadhipok of Siam in the late 1920s, and then began a teaching career in 1933 at St. Mark's School in Southborough, Massachusetts, where a young Robert Lowell was one of his students. During World War II, he served as an aerial gunnery officer in the navy. Following the war, he taught at many universities, including Dart-

mouth, where he served as professor of English and poet-in-residence. The
recipient of nearly every major award that a poet can win—the Pulitzer
Prize, the National Book Award, and the Bollingen Prize, among others—
he was the author of more than a dozen books of poetry, including Reading
the Spirit, Burr Oaks, Great Praises, *and* Selected Poems.

Orchard

I.
Lovely were the fruit trees in the evening.
We sat in the automobile all five of us,
Full of the silence of deep grieving,
For tragedy stalked among the fruit trees.

Strongest was the father, of solid years,
Who set his jaw against the coming winter,
Pure, hard, strong, and infinitely gentle
For the worst that evil brings can only kill us.

Most glorious was the mother, beautiful
Who in the middle course of life was stalked
By the stark shape of malignant disease,
And her face was holy white like all desire.

And we three, in our benumbing youngness,
Half afraid to guess at the danger there,
Looked in stillness at the glowing fruit trees,
While tumultuous passions raged in the air.

II.
And the first, the father, with indomitable will
Strove in iron decision, in all human strength
With a powerful complete contempt of defeat,
Six feet of manhood and not a mark of fear.

And the next, the mother, wonderfully mild,
Wise with the wisdom that never changes,

Poured forth her love divinely magnified
We knew not by what imminent despair.

While the older brother and the younger,
Separate, yet placed in the first light
Of brutal recognition, held a trembling sister
Who knew not the trial of fortitude to come.

And in the evening, among the warm fruit trees
All of life and all of death were there,
Of pain unto death, of struggle to endure,
And the strong right of human love was there.

The Groundhog

In June, amid the golden fields,
I saw a groundhog lying dead.
Dead lay he; my senses shook,
And mind outshot our naked frailty.
There lowly in the vigorous summer
His form began its senseless change,
And made my senses waver dim
Seeing nature ferocious in him.
Inspecting close his maggots' might
And seething cauldron of his being,
Half with loathing, half with a strange love,
I poked him with an angry stick.
The fever arose, became a flame
And Vigour circumscribed the skies,
Immense energy in the sun,
And through my frame a sunless trembling.
My stick had done nor good nor harm.
Then stood I silent in the day
Watching the object, as before;
And kept my reverence for knowledge
Trying for control, to be still,
To quell the passion of the blood;

Until I had bent down on my knees
Praying for joy in the sight of decay.
And so I left; and I returned
In Autumn strict of eye, to see
The sap gone out of the groundhog,
But the bony sodden hulk remained.
But the year had lost its meaning,
And in intellectual chains
I lost both love and loathing,
Muted up in the wall of wisdom.
Another summer took the fields again
Massive and burning, full of life,
But when I chanced upon the spot
There was only a little hair left,
And bones bleaching in the sunlight
Beautiful as architecture;
I watched them like a geometer,
And cut a walking stick from a birch.
It has been three years, now.
There is no sign of the groundhog.
I stood there in the whirling summer,
My hand capped a withered heart,
And thought of China and of Greece,
Of Alexander in his tent;
Of Montaigne in his tower,
Of Saint Theresa in her wild lament.

La Crosse at Ninety Miles an Hour

Better to be the rock above the river,
The bluff, brown and age-old sandstone,
Than the broad river winding to the Gulf.

The river looks like world reality
And has the serenity of wide and open things.
It is a river of even ice today.

Winter men in square cold huts have cut
Round holes to fish through: I saw it as a boy.
They have a will to tamper with the river.

Up on the high bluffs nothing but spirit!
It is there I would be, where an Indian scout was
Long ago, now purely imaginary.

It is a useless and heaven-depended place,
Commodious rock to lock the spirit in,
Where it gazes on the river and the land.

Better to be rock-like than river-like;
Water is a symbol will wear us all away.
Rock comes to the same end, more slowly so.

Rock is the wish of the spirit, heavy symbol,
Something to hold to beyond worldly use.
I feel it in my bones, kinship with vision,

And on the brown bluffs above the Mississippi
In the land of my deepest, earliest memories,
Rushing along at ninety miles an hour,

I feel the old elation of the imagination.
Strong talk of the river and the rock.
Small division between the world and spirit.

1945–1965

* * * * *

CARL RAKOSI
(1903–2004)

Carl Rakosi was born in Berlin, Germany, and lived briefly in Baja, Hungary, before coming to the United States in 1910. He attended the University of Wisconsin and the University of Pennsylvania, where he received degrees in English, psychology, and social work. He later worked as a psychotherapist at a number of clinics in New York, Chicago, New Orleans, Houston, and finally Minneapolis, where he lived from 1945 until his death. First published in Ezra Pound's The Exile *in the 1920s, he was briefly associated with the Objectivists, an early 1930s movement in American poetry led by William Carlos Williams, Louis Zukofsky, George Oppen, and others. His books include* Selected Poems, Amulet, *and* Collected Poems.

The Heifer

After the bath she touched her hair
with Orange Leaf and smiled.

"Henry is gone. Who are you?"

Fumous ashwood violins
all night made bright da capo
constant as specific gravity.
So the umbrellas were put away.
We were together on yachts and beaches,
breakfasts on the ocean,
taxis through the Brandenburger Tor.

"Tell me, who are you?"

I am son
of a Hungarian peasant
who fled military service
where the sheep graze
                    under the Carpathians

and the cheese hangs on the rack
and black bread and potato soup
                        was the family meal

who came to America
                        to a steel mill
and a single room
                        in a boarding house

he who lost
                his father's simple power
to touch and smell,
                        untouched by philosophy . . .
the unexpugnable
                        integrity of a heifer
licking its nose. . . .
forever lost   forever lost.

The Old Homestead

As it gets on in years
the third generation
feeling lonely with its children
goes into its darkroom
and develops a picture
of cattle lumbering in
from the timbered pasture
at the end of a summer's day
a century ago
their bags heavy with milk

planting the acre north
of the hoghouse to sweet corn
for late eating with fresh country butter

families visiting from a hundred miles
singing under a shade tree.

Where the road forks at the red barn
and the oak tree has a knot hole
on its north side
the old ones feel at home
hoeing weeds in a little garden
and marveling how things grow
the corn having jumped a foot
over the Fourth of July weekend.

Here four-square on historic legs
on all sides bounded by
(how is this capitalized?)
God and hard work
stands the Nineteenth Century.

. . . .

JOSEPH LANGLAND
(1917–)

Joseph Langland was born in Spring Grove, Minnesota, of Norwegian ances-
try, and raised in Iowa. Educated at Santa Ana College and the University of
Iowa, he taught at the University of Wyoming and the University of Massa-
chusetts at Amherst, where he founded the Masters of Fine Arts Program in
Creative Writing. His books include The Green Town, The Wheel
of Summer *(recipient of the Melville Cane Award),* The Sacrifice Po-
ems, Any Body's Song *(a National Poetry Series selection),* Twelve
Poems with Preludes and Postludes, *and* Selected Poems.

In 1912, My Father Buys the Victor Record of 'Sextet from Lucia' from Hoegh's Jewelry Store in a Small Town in Minnesota

Charley is entering the record and jewelry store now,
a dapper forty-one, just married to his elegant Clara,

with nine children still to be conceived and carried and born and raised clear into the Depression. He has just come from the bank, smartly dressed in his tight waistcoat and dark striped trousers. As he enters the door, Ove Hoegh glances up with appreciation: a favorite, a good customer, a friend.

Yes, indeed, he has some new records from the operas: Alma Gluck, some more Caruso, Louise Homer, Journet, Amati, even Melba, and a new quartet from *Rigoletto*. But Charley, I want you to hear this! Ove winds the Victrola, shining in polished oak. My father leans lightly against the jeweled counter and stands on his left foot, with his right balanced across it on the tip of its toe; his right elbow is on the counter, his left hand in his pocket. His head turns slightly outward into the room; he tips it ever so slightly down for listening.

Then the seven-dollar twelve-inch seventy-eight with its red-and-gold heart begins to turn. The shining steel needle, with a soft swish, slowly negotiates the black edge into the deep grooves, and the arpeggio chordal plucking in the strings begins. And then the huge horn hidden in the box behind its fine brocade begins softly singing: sol sol SOL, do MI re DO SOL in its vibrant Italian vowels. The little gallery is transfixed. Waves of harmonic melodies float up and over, interweave, making their exits and entering again with violins and rapiers and satin gowns. All their songs gesture in embroidered pantaloons and waxed moustaches; pale hands sweep over their troubled foreheads; they implore the air; they brace themselves on their hips, indignant, wan, robust, judicious, serene, over the carved table and the velvet and leather chairs.

Oh, my father is a fine man now, there in that royal box with all that splendid company! His skull is the philharmonic of them all, jeweled with sound.

And when intermission comes, he will step out on Main Street and all along down Division, to greet his Clara Elizabeth with an amulet under his arms to tell her, like a messenger from on high, that La Scala has finally come—Sembrich, Caruso, Scotti, Journet, Severina and Daddi—all the way from Milano to Spring Grove, Minnesota, and he is bringing them home.

.   .   .   .

REED WHITTEMORE
(1919–)

Reed Whittemore was born in New Haven, Connecticut, and educated at Yale and Princeton. The author of numerous books of poetry, short stories, essays, and literary biographies, including Heroes and Heroines, The Boy from Iowa, Poems New and Selected, *and* The Past, The Future, The Present, *he served as literary editor of* The New Republic *and twice as Consultant in Poetry to the Library of Congress. From 1946 to 1965, he taught English at Carleton College in Northfield, where he edited the literary journal* Furioso, *which later became* The Carleton Miscellany.

The Fall of the House of Usher

It was a big boxy wreck of a house
Owned by a classmate of mine named Rod Usher,
Who lived in the thing with his twin sister.
He was a louse and she was a souse.

While I was visiting them one wet summer, she died.
We buried her,
Or rather we stuck her in a back room for a bit, meaning to
    bury her
When the graveyard dried.

But the weather got wetter.
One night we were both waked by a twister,
Plus a screeching and howling outside that turned out to be
    sister
Up and dying again, making it hard for Rod to forget her.

He didn't. He and she died in a heap, and I left quick,
Which was lucky since the house fell in right after,

                                    Like a ton of brick.

The High School Band in September

On warm days in September the high school band
Is up with the birds and marches along our street,
Boom boom,
To a field where it goes boom boom until eight forty-five
When it marches, as in the old rhyme, back, boom boom,
To its study halls, leaving our street
Empty except for the leaves that descend to no drum
And lie still.
In September
A great many high school bands beat a great many drums,
And the silences after their partings are very deep.

When Father Left in the Morning

When father left in the morning
He had the mark of evening

On him, but at evening the evening
Was wholly evening.
He lay with forever
After supper.

Mother watched him
From the other bed,
Brushing her hair back, looking for slippers,
Smoking.
Somewhere out in the hall
Were the living. She was ill.

The moon revolved
Over East Rock Road.
The Packard sat by the curb.
I lay in my bed in the next room
Listening,
Waiting for news.

But the news in the evening
Was always the same news,
And in the morning
The drift was to evening.
I was grown
Before morning came.

.   .   .   .

ADRIEN STOUTENBURG
(1916–1982)

Adrien Stoutenburg was born in Darfur, Minnesota, and attended the Min-
neapolis School of Art. Upon graduation, she was employed at the Hennepin
County Library and the Richfield News *before moving to California to*
work as a political reporter, a librarian, and an editor for Parnassus Press in

Berkeley. She published more than thirty-five children's books, as well as books of poetry, fiction, and nonfiction. Her poetry collections include Heroes, Advise Us *(winner of the Lamont Poetry Award)*, Short History of the Fur Trade *(recipient of the California Commonwealth Club Award for Poetry)*, *and* Greenwich Mean Time. *Other awards include two Poetry Society of America Awards, the Helen Bollis Award in Poetry from* Poetry Northwest, *and nine Borestone Mountain Awards in Poetry.*

Cicada

I lay with my heart under me,
under the white sun,
face down to fields
and a life that gleamed
under my palm like an emerald hinge.
I sheltered him where we lay alive
under the body of the sun.
Trees there dropped their shadows
like black fruit,
and the thin-necked sparrows came
crying through the light.

At my life line I felt
his bent, bright knee
work like a latch.
He was safe with me
in the room my round bones made—
or might have been—
but he sang like a driven nail
and his skinless eyes looked out,
wanting himself as he was.

Wisdom was imprecise,
my hand's loose judgement dark.
Some jewel work straining in his thigh

broke like a kingdom.
I let him go,
a jackstraw limping to the dynamo
of hunger under the hungering sun
and the world's quick gizzard.
High noon hummed,
all parts in place—
or nearly so.

Mote

The hummingbird, acquaintance,
hanging at the feeder,
fencing with his beak,
suspended as by whirling arms
or two round harps,
is instant color.

Here we have a minute thunder,
mandolin, banjo, fever,
potential crisis of motion
as in a spinning jenny
grown eccentric, its cotton raveling
into a knot like a flower.

This spinner ends in rainbow,
and so begins.
(The inside of the egg, surely,
is a centrifuge of opals.)

He rests, rarely and neatly,
after his spike explores
honey trapped in glass and jasmine.
He goes to that rest so swiftly
he is nearly a myth. He becomes

a bud on a twig of a bough.
He dives into wind as into water.
He lifts himself, or is lifted,
into a feathered diamond
greener than the leaves
he brings his light to.

He is an uncertain visitor,
unpredictable, fickle, late to appointments,
obsessed with nectar in distant cabinets.

But when he comes, shining the window,
and leans there, gleams in his cape,
tips his javelin and remains,
we lay down our books, music, cards,
and watch like the cats
who are also our boarders,
as helpless as they
to stay that mote by talons or love.

Interior Decoration

I am thinking of doing over my room,
of plastering wings on it,
of letting clouds in through the attic,
of collecting moles
and training them to assemble in an oval
for a rug as bright as black water:
of growing orchids under the couch
    for a lavender surprise
    against the sleeping dust;
of inviting wind to the closet—
    empty shapes will blow and sing like sails—
of planting a quail's nest in a yellow corner—
    eggs in time will hatch out stumbling flowers—
of taking a fox for a companion—
    his fur will be my fire on cold days—

of building a great square silo of books:
    pale green, blue (moss color, sky color),
    deep red, russet, orange (sun and blowing leaf color),
    their spines scrawled with loud gold
    and chiming silver—ARABIA DESERTA,
    LETTERS OF RILKE, WALDEN, HUNGER,
    BEYOND GOOD AND EVIL.
These, when the blizzard comes,
will be my soaring walls.

. . . .

JOHN BERRYMAN
(1914–1972)

John Berryman's many books include the poetry collections Homage to Mistress Bradstreet, 77 Dream Songs, Delusions, Etc., *and* Collected Poems 1937–1971, *as well as collections of fiction and essays. Born in Oklahoma and educated at Columbia and Cambridge, he taught at Brown, Harvard, and Princeton universities, and was the recipient of numerous honors and awards for his work, including Rockefeller and Guggenheim fellowships, the 1965 Pulitzer Prize, and the 1969 National Book Award. A renowned teacher of literature, he came to the University of Minnesota in 1955 and taught there until his suicide in 1972.*

The Ball Poem

What is the boy now, who has lost his ball,
What, what is he to do? I saw it go
Merrily bouncing, down the street, and then
Merrily over—there it is in the water!
No use to say 'O there are other balls':
An ultimate shaking grief fixes the boy
As he stands rigid, trembling, staring down
All his young days into the harbour where

His ball went. I would not intrude on him,
A dime, another ball, is worthless. Now
He senses first responsibility
In a world of possessions. People will take balls,
Balls will be lost always, little boy,
And no one buys a ball back. Money is external.
He is learning, well behind his desperate eyes,
The epistemology of loss, how to stand up
Knowing what every man must one day know
And most know many days, how to stand up.
And gradually light returns to the street,
A whistle blows, the ball is out of sight,
Soon part of me will explore the deep and dark
Floor of the harbour . . . I am everywhere,
I suffer and move, my mind and my heart move
With all that move me, under the water
Or whistling, I am not a little boy.

from *77 Dream Songs*

Life, friends, is boring. We must not say so.
After all, the sky flashes, the great sea yearns,
we ourselves flash and yearn,
and moreover my mother told me as a boy
(repeatingly) 'Ever to confess you're bored
means you have no

Inner Resources.' I conclude now I have no
inner resources, because I am heavy bored.
Peoples bore me,
literature bores me, especially great literature,
Henry bores me, with his plights & gripes
as bad as achilles,

who loves people and valiant art, which bores me.
And the tranquil hills, & gin, look like a drag

and somehow a dog
has taken itself & its tail considerably away
into mountains or sea or sky, leaving
behind: me, wag.

Henry's Understanding

He was reading late, at Richard's, down in Maine,
aged 32? Richard & Helen long in bed,
my good wife long in bed.
All I had to do was strip & get into my bed,
putting the marker in the book, & sleep,
& wake to a hot breakfast.

Off the coast was an island, P'tit Manaan,
the bluff from Richard's lawn was almost sheer.
A chill at four o'clock.
It only takes a few minutes to make a man.
A concentration upon now & here.
Suddenly, unlike Bach,

& horribly, unlike Bach, it occurred to me
that *one* night, instead of warm pajamas,
I'd take off all my clothes
& cross the damp cold lawn & down the bluff
into the terrible water & walk forever
under it out toward the island.

Of Suicide

Reflexions on suicide, & on my father, possess me.
I drink too much. My wife threatens separation.
She won't 'nurse' me. She feels 'inadequate'.
We don't mix together.

It's an hour later in the East.
I could call up Mother in Washington, D.C.
But could she help me?
And all this postal adulation & reproach?

A basis rock-like of love & friendship
for all this world-wide madness seems to be needed.
Epictetus is in some ways my favourite philosopher.
Happy men have died earlier.

I still plan to go to Mexico this summer.
The Olmec images! Chichén Itzá!
D. H. Lawrence has a wild dream of it.
Malcolm Lowry's book when it came out I taught to
　　my precept at Princeton.

I don't entirely resign. I may teach the Third Gospel
this afternoon. I haven't made up my mind.
It seems to me sometimes that others have easier jobs
& do them worse.

Well, we must labour & dream. Gogol was impotent,
somebody in Pittsburgh told me.
I said: At what age? They couldn't answer.
That is a damned serious matter.

Rembrandt was sober. There we differ. Sober.
Terrors came on him. To us too they come.
Of suicide I continually think.
Apparently he didn't. I'll teach Luke.

.   .   .   .

ROBERT BLY
(1926–)

Robert Bly was born in Madison, Minnesota, and educated at St. Olaf College, Harvard, and the University of Iowa. One of the most influential poets, translators, editors, and publishers of his generation, he is the author of dozens of books, including Silence in the Snowy Fields, The Light Around the Body, Eating the Honey of Words: New and Selected Poems, *and* The Night Abraham Called to the Stars. *In the 1950s, he founded and coedited with William Duffy the literary journal and small press* The Fifties *(later known successively as* The Sixties *and* The Seventies*). Among his many awards are the 1968 National Book Award, the Ruth Lilly Prize, the Minnesota Humanities Prize for Literature, and a Minnesota State Book Award. He lives in Minneapolis.*

Driving Toward the Lac Qui Parle River

I
I am driving; it is dusk; Minnesota.
The stubble field catches the last growth of sun.
The soybeans are breathing on all sides.
Old men are sitting before their houses on car seats
In the small towns. I am happy,
The moon rising above the turkey sheds.

II
The small world of the car
Plunges through the deep fields of the night,
On the road from Willmar to Milan.
This solitude covered with iron
Moves through the fields of night
Penetrated by the noise of crickets.

III
Nearly to Milan, suddenly a small bridge,
And water kneeling in the moonlight.

In small towns the houses are built right on the ground;
The lamplight falls on all fours in the grass.
When I reach the river, the full moon covers it;
A few people are talking low in a boat.

After Drinking All Night with a Friend,
We Go Out in a Boat at Dawn
to See Who Can Write the Best Poem

These pines, these fall oaks, these rocks,
This water dark and touched by wind—
I am like you, you dark boat,
Drifting over water fed by cool springs.

Beneath the waters, since I was a boy,
I have dreamt of strange and dark treasures,
Not of gold or strange stones, but the true
Gift, beneath the pale lakes of Minnesota.

This morning also, drifting in the dawn wind,
I sense my hands, and my shoes, and this ink—
Drifting, as all of the body drifts,
Above the clouds of the flesh and the stone.

A few friendships, a few dawns, a few glimpses of grass,
A few oars weathered by the snow and the heat,
So we drift toward shore, over cold waters,
No longer caring if we drift or go straight.

The Resemblance Between Your Life and a Dog

I never intended to have this life, believe me—
It just happened. You know how dogs turn up
At a farm, and they wag but don't explain.

It's good if you can accept your life—you'll notice
Your face has become deranged trying to adjust
To it. Your face thought your life would look

Like your bedroom mirror when you were ten.
That was a clear river touched by mountain wind.
Even your parents can't believe how much you've changed.

Sparrows in winter, if you've ever held one, all feathers,
Burst out of your hand with a fiery glee.
You see them later in hedges. Teachers praise you,

But you can't quite get back to the winter sparrow.
Your life is a dog. He's been hungry for miles,
Doesn't particularly like you, but gives up, and comes in.

Stealing Sugar from the Castle

We are poor students who stay after school to study joy.
We are like those birds in the India mountains.
I am a widow whose child is her only joy.

The only thing I hold in my ant-like head
Is the builder's plan of the castle of sugar.
Just to steal one grain of sugar is a joy!

Like a bird, we fly out of darkness into the hall,
Which is lit with singing, then fly out again.
Being shut out of the warm hall is also a joy.

I am a laggard, a loafer, and an idiot. But I love
To read about those who caught one glimpse
Of the Face, and died twenty years later in joy.

I don't mind your saying I will die soon.
Even in the sound of the word soon, I hear
The word you which begins every sentence of joy.

"You're a thief!" the judge said. "Let's see
Your hands!" I showed my callused hands in court.
My sentence was a thousand years of joy.

.   .   .   .

JAMES WRIGHT
(1927–1980)

Born in Martin's Ferry, Ohio, James Wright was educated at Kenyon College and the University of Washington, and attended the University of Vienna as a Fulbright Scholar. He was the author of numerous books of poetry, including The Green Wall *(recipient of the Yale Series of Younger Poets Award),* Collected Poems *(winner of the 1972 Pulitzer Prize),* The Branch Will Not Break, *and* Above the River: The Complete Poems. *From 1957 to 1963, he taught at the University of Minnesota and from 1963 to 1965 at Macalester College.*

Lying in a Hammock at William Duffy's Farm in Pine Island, Minnesota

Over my head, I see the bronze butterfly,
Asleep on the black trunk,
Blowing like a leaf in green shadow.
Down the ravine behind the empty house,
The cowbells follow one another
Into the distances of the afternoon.
To my right,
In a field of sunlight between two pines,
The droppings of last year's horses
Blaze up into golden stones.
I lean back, as the evening darkens and comes on.
A chicken hawk floats over, looking for home.
I have wasted my life.

A Blessing

Just off the highway to Rochester, Minnesota,
Twilight bounds softly forth on the grass.
And the eyes of those two Indian ponies
Darken with kindness.
They have come gladly out of the willows
To welcome my friend and me.
We step over the barbed wire into the pasture
Where they have been grazing all day, alone.
They ripple tensely, they can hardly contain their happiness
That we have come.
They bow shyly as wet swans. They love each other.
There is no loneliness like theirs.
At home once more,
They begin munching the young tufts of spring in the
    darkness.
I would like to hold the slenderer one in my arms,
For she has walked over to me
And nuzzled my left hand.
She is black and white,
Her mane falls wild on her forehead,
And the light breeze moves me to caress her long ear
That is delicate as the skin over a girl's wrist.
Suddenly I realize
That if I stepped out of my body I would break
Into blossom.

The Minneapolis Poem

to John Logan

1
I wonder how many old men last winter
Hungry and frightened by namelessness prowled
The Mississippi shore
Lashed blind by the wind, dreaming

Of suicide in the river.
The police remove their cadavers by daybreak
And turn them in somewhere.
Where?
How does the city keep lists of its fathers
Who have no names?
By Nicollet Island I gaze down at the dark water
So beautifully slow.
And I wish my brothers good luck
And a warm grave.

2
The Chippewa young men
Stab one another shrieking
Jesus Christ.
Split-lipped homosexuals limp in terror of assault.
High school backfields search under benches
Near the Post Office. Their faces are the rich
Raw bacon without eyes.
The Walker Art Center crowd stare
At the Guthrie Theater.

3
Tall Negro girls from Chicago
Listen to light songs.
They know when the supposed patron
Is a plainclothesman.
A cop's palm
Is a roach dangling down the scorched fangs
Of a light bulb.
The soul of a cop's eyes
Is an eternity of Sunday daybreak in the suburbs
Of Juárez, Mexico.

4
The legless beggars are gone, carried away
By white birds.

The Artificial Limbs Exchange is gutted
And sown with lime.
The whalebone crutches and hand-me-down trusses
Huddle together dreaming in a desolation
Of dry groins.
I think of poor men astonished to waken
Exposed in broad daylight by the blade
Of a strange plough.

5
All over the walls of comb cells
Automobiles perfumed and blindered
Consent with a mutter of high good humor
To take their two naps a day.
Without sound windows glide back
Into dusk.
The sockets of a thousand blind bee graves tier upon tier
Tower not quite toppling.
There are men in this city who labor dawn after dawn
To sell me my death.

6
But I could not bear
To allow my poor brother my body to die
In Minneapolis.
The old man Walt Whitman our countryman
Is now in America our country
Dead.
But he was not buried in Minneapolis
At least.
And no more may I be
Please God.

7
I want to be lifted up
By some great white bird unknown to the police,
And soar for a thousand miles and be carefully hidden

Modest and golden as one last corn grain,
Stored with the secrets of the wheat and the mysterious
     lives
Of the unnamed poor.

.   .   .   .

Thomas McGrath
(1916 1990)

Thomas McGrath was born on a North Dakota farm and educated at the
University of North Dakota, Louisiana State, and Oxford University,
where he was a Rhodes Scholar. After serving in the Aleutian Islands of
Alaska in World War II, he worked as a scriptwriter in Hollywood until he
was blacklisted for his left-wing political convictions. Cofounder and first ed-
itor of the literary journal Crazyhorse, *he worked as a freelance writer*
and taught at various schools, including Moorhead State University in
Moorhead, Minnesota. Awards and honors for his work included two Bush
Foundation Fellowships, a Guggenheim Fellowship, an NEA Senior Fellow-
ship, the Shelley Memorial Award, the Lenore Marshall/Nation Prize for
Poetry, and a Minnesota Book Award. His volumes of poetry include Let-
ter to an Imaginary Friend, The Movie at the End of the
World: Collected Poems, Death Song, *and* Passages Toward
the Dark.

Praises

The vegetables please us with their modes and virtues.
                                        The demure heart
Of the lettuce inside its circular court, baroque ear
Of quiet under its rustling house of lace, pleases
Us.
     And the bold strength of the celery, its green Hispanic
!Shout! its exclamatory confetti.

                                   And the analogue that is Onion:
Ptolemaic astronomy and tearful allegory, the Platonic
     circles
Of His inexhaustible soul!
                                   O and the straightforwardness
In the labyrinth of Cabbage, the infallible rectitude of
     Homegrown Mushroom
Under its cone of silence like a papal hat—
                                   All these
Please us.
             And the syllabus of the corn,
                                   that wampum,
                                             its golden
Roads leading out of the wigwams of its silky and youthful
     smoke;
The nobility of the dill, cool in its silences and cathedrals;
Tomatoes five-alarm fires in their musky barrios, peas
Asleep in their cartridge clips,
                                   beetsblood,
                                   colonies of the imperial
Cauliflower, and the buddha-like seeds of the pepper
Turning their prayerwheels in the green gloom of their
     caves.
All these we praise: they please us all ways: these smallest
     virtues.
All these earth-given:
                    and the heaven-hung fruit also . . .
                                   As instance
Banana which continually makes angelic ears out of sour
Purses, or the winy abacus of the holy grape on its cross
Of alcohol, or the peach with its fur like a young girl's—
All these we praise: the winter in the flesh of the apple, and
     the sun
Domesticated under the orange's rind.
                                   We praise
By the skin of our teeth, Persimmon, and Pawpaw's constant
Affair with gravity, and the proletariat of the pomegranate

Inside its leathery city.
                    And let us praise all these
As they please us: skin, flesh, flower, and the flowering
Bones of their seeds: from which come orchards: bees:
    honey:
Flowers, love's language, love, heart's ease, poems, praise.

The Bread of This World; Praises III

On the Christmaswhite plains of the floured and flowering
    kitchen table
The holy loaves of the bread are slowly being born:
Rising like low hills in the steepled pastures of light—
Lifting the prairie farmhouse afternoon on their arching
    backs.

It must be Friday, the bread tells us as it climbs
Out of itself like a poor man climbing up on a cross
Toward transfiguration.
                    And it is a Mystery, surely,
If we think that this bread rises only out of the enigma
That leavens the Apocalypse of yeast, or ascends on the
    beards and beads
Of a rosary and priesthood of barley those Friday heavens
Lofting . . .

            But we who will eat the bread when we come in
Out of the cold and dark know it is a deeper mystery
That brings the bread to rise:
                            it is the love and faith
Of large and lonely women, moving like floury clouds
In farmhouse kitchens, that rounds the loaves and the lives
Of those around them . . .
                    just as we know it is hunger—
Our own and others'—that gives all salt and savor to bread.

But that is a workaday story and this is the end of the week.

The End of the World

The end of the world: it was given to me to see it.
Came in the black dark, a bulge in the starless sky,
A trembling at the heart of the night, a twitching of the
 webby flesh of the earth.
And out of the bowels of the street one beastly,
 ungovernable cry.

Came and I recognized it: the end of the world.
And waited for the lightless plunge, the fury splitting the
 rock.
And waited: a kissing of leaves: a whisper of man-killing
 ancestral night—
Then: a tinkle of music, laughter from the next block.

Yet waited still: for the awful traditional fire,
Hearing mute thunder, the long collapse of sky.
It falls forever. But no one noticed. The end of the world
 provoked
Out of the dark a single and melancholy sigh

From my neighbor who sat on his porch drinking beer
 in the dark.
No: I was not God's prophet. Armageddon was never
And always: this night in the poor street where a careless
 irreverent laughter
Postpones the end of the world: in which we live forever.

1965–1985

♦   ♦   ♦   ♦

PHEBE HANSON
(1928–)

Born in Sacred Heart, Minnesota, and educated at Augsburg College, Phebe Hanson had a long and illustrious teaching career. Spanning forty years, it began in a one-room country school, continued through many years of teaching high school English, and ended with fifteen years at the Minneapolis College of Art and Design, from which she retired as Associate Professor Emeritus. The recipient of a Bush Foundation Fellowship and a Jerome Minnesota Center for the Book Arts Grant, she is the author of Sacred Hearts *and* Why Still Dance.

First Car

Here he is in an old photo album,
my Norwegian immigrant father,
newly-ordained graduate of Augsburg Seminary.
My first car—1926,
he has written under the boxy Model T,
familiar car like a child's drawing,
home-made looking,
a car so simple even a child
could drive it,
and I used to pretend,
perched on Daddy's lap,
while we sat in the driveway
waiting for Mother.
Darling and doted-upon first child,
I was stuffed into elaborate costumes,
hair curled and beribboned,
safe in the front seat
between Mother and Daddy,
who drove us to his churches in the country,
Camp Release and Black Oak Lake.
We sang together on the way,
I'll be a sunbeam for Jesus,

I'll shine for Him each day,
In every way try to please Him,
At home and school and play,
that winter night, bitter cold,
snow hissing against our windshield,
the only car out in the midnight storm.
Our dashboard burst into flame;
Daddy disturbed my cozy sleep
against Mother's arm
to rush us out of the car
to stand on the shoulder, hoping
for someone to stop.
That image of the three of us remains,
minister father in long black coat,
mother with fur collar surrounding her face,
child in blue snowsuit and aviator helmet,
as if we were posing for a studio portrait,
as if the swirling snow and relentless wind
were fake backdrops in those old photographs
where the faces radiate a strange silvery light,
and the eyes seem to know that death's ahead
from tuberculosis, pneumonia, diphtheria.
We still stand in the bright blizzard light,
frozen images by the side of the road.
I don't remember what happened next.
I don't remember ever being rescued.

Santa Lucia

December, 1938
and my grandparents
give their yearly party
at the church where
my grandfather is janitor.
Everyone comes to honor
Lucia, strange saint

for Swedes, virgin & martyr
of Syracuse, whose fiancé
denounced her
when she became a Christian
ordered boiling oil
and burning pitch
poured over her
stubborn head,
but on this night
I am 10,
know nothing
of that other Lucia,
know only I
get to put on the long white choir robe
tied with red satin sash,
get to wear the crown of candles
that remind everyone
of the light she brought
when she appeared
to Swedish peasants
during a famine.
I am afraid
as Grandma lights
the candles
in the crown on my head,
that the flames
will catch my hair on fire,
but I walk in slowly
head held straight,
carrying a tray of *lussekatter*
and deliver pieces of the bread
to all the Swedes
gathered in Gloria Dei Lutheran Church
that long-ago December night
just before the world
burst into flames.

.   .   .   .

ALVIN GREENBERG
(1932–)

Born in Cincinnati, Ohio, and educated at the University of Cincinnati and the University of Washington, Alvin Greenberg is the author of four novels, four collections of short stories, two books of nonfiction, and nine volumes of poetry, including Hurry Back, Why We Live With Animals, Heavy Wings, *and* Metaform. *Among his many honors and awards are two National Endowment for the Arts Fellowships, two Bush Foundation Fellowships, and the Loft-McKnight Award of Distinction in Poetry. Former editor of the literary journal* The Minnesota Review, *he served as professor of English at Macalester College from 1965 until his retirement in 2002.*

freight train, freight train

all freight, the sudden trains that uncouple my passage
    home
like flash floods, stranding me in these winter afternoon
    rains
counting carloads of lumber, flatcars of heavy equipment,
    sealed
boxcars headed out of the city, cities themselves, miles long
and full of industry, but with only a grim mayor at the
    throttle
and a handful of sleepy maintenance workers for
    inhabitants:
where have all the passengers, all the rightful citizens, gone?

in 1940, in the dazed center of my childhood and the last
    year
before the war—*our* war—we watched my suited, suitcased
    father
descend the tiled concourse to board "the james whitcomb
    riley"
at cincinnati's brand-new, brassy, domed and cavernous, art-

decoed union terminal with its floor-to-ceiling mosaics of
    labor
and industry. almost empty even then, it echoed with the
    hard
departures of newsstands, shoeshine boys, our own hurried
    heels
on the marble floors. then it was troop trains, troop trains,
all troop trains: the long, thrilling, khaki freight of the war.

but what did we know of trains then? of industrious
    engineers
hauling their boxcars of battered freight across the
    cavernous
wastes of europe to stoke the engines of empire like so much
kindling? of winters thick with the smoke of coal and flesh?
no wonder we take to the air now, or sit in our cars,
    dreaming,
while the long cities of the dead roll by. somewhere, even
    then,
there must have been a citizen stopped at a level crossing on a
winter day just like this, motor turned off to save the
    precious
fuel, counting the rattling box cars, thick with the nostalgia
only these cold rains can bring, ignorant, dreaming of trains.

cutting birch

like yourself at the head of the stairs with your hand
on the wobbly old banister, even the trees may take
their own sweet time coming down, no matter you've
cut them through. and those birds up there as well,
all of them dressed according to sex and season,
in their impeccable layers of altitude may linger
awhile. yes, and the dog in his yellow slicker and
webbed feet for the moment stays dry, who'd otherwise
gladly fetch you a stick out of anything short of ice

but balks here on the steep beach at the slap and suck
of the waves, though wet is wet as far as i can tell,
and sky is sky, a landing at the top of the stairs,
a roomful of gravity, no matter how wide or how high,
in which all falling bodies must obey identical laws.

though you might not know it to see their clever gy-
rations or to listen to all their varied, birdlike cries
—to yourself and the dog and the saw and the birch
singing in harmony here at the head of the stairs—
nothing, not even tomorrow's distant, dubious sunrise,
is more predictable than a falling body as it falls.

as we, too, grow older

suddenly all the parents have taken up dying,
this one of several cancers, that one by the heart,
by stroke, my own father of forgetfulness: one
by one the parents moving back in with the children
and the children feeding them, often by hand,
getting up at night to take them to the bathroom
as day by day the parents recede from the world
the way the world recedes from my father's mind
who once traveled it as if he owned it all
but now lets it slip through his fingers
like his shoestrings, not remembering what's
connected to what, or how, the great loop
of his life coming untied and he can't recall
what goes where, wanders out with laces loose
and dragging, stumbles over them, of course,
on the top step, plunging downward, arms out,
where we, who saw this happening, catch him,
he floats gently into our arms, laces trailing,
almost as if there's no one there, yes, as if
he's forgotten how he's weighed on us all these years.

. . . .

James L. White
(1936–1981)

Born in Indianapolis, Indiana, James L. White began his training as a classical ballet dancer at the age of sixteen and was awarded a scholarship to the American Ballet Theater School. He then danced for ten years in the United States and Germany. He was educated at universities in Indiana and Colorado, then came to Minnesota to develop a creative writing program for Native American children through the Minnesota Writers-in-the-Schools Program. He was the author of The Salt Ecstasies, The Del Rio Hotel, A Crow's Story of Deer, *and* Divorce Proceedings.

from *Gatherings*

NEW LIGHT
I've been dying to go back
through dust, hymns, and the photos of death.
The Union Station sleeps like a defunct whale
and I join its echoing space to think of caskets settling.
I've returned to dust where the peeling signs read:
REMEMBER ALL DEPARTURES ARE CHANGEABLE
BE SURE YOU ARE IN THE CORRECT TIME
I want to sleep now
in an afternoon dream pushing 'now' away to die completely
as stone or heart
or rising wind.

I want to dream beyond this aloneness,
to feel him carry me through the wind that is rising.
My father in his white strolling suit.
I ride his shoulders into the greening
light of this damp time.

We take flowers in the morning,
my father, bold as God,
mother in her withering step,

in her withering white,
and me in boyhood with a sword of lilacs.

In this dream my people live forever.
We carry the flowers of waltzing light
into a rising wind, through into spring.

We, who are going on a trip.

An Ordinary Composure

I question what poetry will tremble the wall into
hearing or tilt the stone angel's slight wings at words
of the past like a memory caught in elms. We see
nothing ahead. My people and I lean against great
medical buildings with news of our predicted death,
and give up mostly between one and three in the
morning, never finding space large enough for a true
departure, so our eyes gaze earthward, wanting to say
something simple as *the meal's too small: I want more.* Then
we empty from a room on Intensive Care into the
sea, releasing our being into the slap of waves.

Poems break down here at the thought of arms never
coupling into full moons by holding those we love
again, and so we resort to the romantic: a white horse
set quivering like a slab of marble into dancing flesh.

Why remember being around a picnic table over at
Brookside Park? We played softball that afternoon.
My mother wore her sweater even in the summer be-
cause of the diabetes. Night blackened the lake like a
caught breath. We packed things up. I think I was go-
ing to school that fall or a job somewhere. Michael'd
go to Korea. Before we left I hit the torn softball into
the lake and Michael said, 'You can't do that for shit
James Lee.'

Going back I realized the picnic was for us. It started
raining in a totally different way, knowing we'd grow
right on up into wars and trains and deaths and lov-
ing people and leaving them and being left and being
alone.

That's the way of my life, the ordinary composure of
loving, loneliness and death, and too these prayers at
the waves, the white horse shimmering, bringing it
toward us out of coldest marble.

. . . .

BILL HOLM
(1943–)

The grandson of Icelandic immigrant farmers, poet and essayist Bill Holm
was born and raised in Minneota and was educated at Gustavus Adolphus
College and the University of Kansas. He is the author of numerous books
of poetry, essays, travel, and memoirs, including Coming Home Crazy,
The Dead Get By with Everything, Playing Haydn for the
Angel of Death, *and* Eccentric Islands: Travels Real and Imag-
inary. *The recipient of a Fulbright Fellowship, a Bush Foundation Fellow-*
ship, a National Endowment for the Arts Fellowship, and a Minnesota Book
Award, he lives in Minneota and teaches at Southwest Minnesota State Uni-
versity in Marshall.

The Icelandic Language

In this language, no industrial revolution;
no pasteurized milk; no oxygen, no telephone;
only sheep, fish, horses, water falling.
The middle class can hardly speak it.

In this language, no flush toilet; you stumble
through dark and rain with a handful of rags.
The door groans; the old smell comes
up from under the earth to meet you.

But this language believes in ghosts;
chairs rock by themselves under the lamp; horses
neigh inside an empty gully, nothing
at the bottom but moonlight and black rocks.

The woman with marble hands whispers
this language to you in your sleep; faces
come to the window and sing rhymes; old ladies
wind long hair, hum, tat, fold jam inside pancakes.

In this language, you can't chit-chat
holding a highball in your hand, can't
even be polite. Once the sentence starts its course,
all your grief and failure come clear at last.

Old inflections move from case to case,
gender to gender, softening consonants, darkening
vowels, till they sound like the sea moving
icebergs back and forth in its mouth.

At the Icelandic Emigration Center in Hofsós

Says the old Icelander
choosing carefully his English words:
"If it had been then as it is now
your grandfather would never have left."
"No," I nod, looking around the parking lot,
but think only silently: Give a man
a big Toyota, a cell phone, a debit card,
and he won't go anywhere.
"No, he would not have left," I say aloud.

"And I would have been born here
where I could have caused trouble
in Icelandic, and not English."
He thinks this is witty, so he laughs,
probably thinks I have inherited
Icelandic humor. What trouble
could anyone cause here
where trouble left so long ago,
leaving the open hole where money
could flow into the harbor like the tide
lifting all the gleaming boats
a little nearer heaven?

The Icelandic Emigration to Minneota, Minnesota

I
After only a thousand years where they were,
In Vopnafjördur, Floi and Jökulldal,
They left again, some for coffee, some for land,
Some no doubt for the hell of it, and came here.
They did not keep slaves, did not get capital,
Did not open any more wilderness. They farmed,
Grumbled, voted Republican, said their Rs wrong,
Dreamed in genders. A few went out to the barn
With ropes, but from another few it dropped away
So quickly that after a few years you could
Not tell them from the others. By the next
Generation the names went wrong in the neighbors'
Mouths; the R slipped off the teeth, and slid back
Into the throat. The dreams came in genders now
Only after whiskey, or when the last disease
Fastened its baling hook deep into the brain.

II
In the third generation, all that was left:
Sweet cake, small stories, a few words whose meaning

Slunk away to die under the mental stone
That buries all the lost languages in America.
The Mayans are there, Pequod and Penobscot,
And the Mandingo, and the Delaware Swedes.
The first tongue lost, did they acquire another?
The language of marketing and deterring
For the language of fish, poverty and poems?
In *The Invasion of the Body Snatchers*,
Seed pods open in your own closet at night,
Metastasizing into a body in-
distinguishable from your own, but the brain
Is something new, without memory, without
Passion, without you. Is this what it's like
To become a whole American at last?

.   .   .   .

PHILIP DACEY
(1939–)

Philip Dacey was born in St. Louis, Missouri, and holds degrees from St. Louis University, Stanford University, and the University of Iowa. The recipient of two National Endowment for the Arts Fellowships, three Pushcart Prizes, a Bush Foundation Fellowship, and a Loft-McKnight Fellowship in Poetry, he is the author of eight volumes of poetry, including The Deathbed Playboy, How I Escaped the Labyrinth and Other Poems, The Boy Under the Bed, *and* The Night Shift in the Crucifix Factory, *and coeditor of* Strong Measures: Contemporary American Poetry in Traditional Forms. *In 2004, he moved from Marshall, where he had taught for thirty-five years at Southwest Minnesota State University, to New York City.*

from *Coal*

TROY
1,122 pop. . . . dependent largely on local coal mines.
The WPA Guide to Illinois, 1939

My grandfather mined
for coal in southern
Illinois. I never met him.
My father remembers him
coming home black
with dust, never
getting it all off.
In church, the cleaned-up
miners could be told
from the other men
by the coal dust still
in creases around their eyes,
rings of dark beauty
many women would envy.
His young wife dead,
my grandfather would have
dressed four sons in their
Sunday best and told them
to stay clean outside
while he dressed himself.
And once he carried my father,
broken leg dangling,
down Donk's Row,
their street, named
for the donkeys that pulled
the cars in the mine
and that my father saw
on his way to school,
dead, tossed
in the dust by the entrance
underground, becoming dust

themselves
to be carried away.
I love to say
my grandfather mined for coal
in southern Illinois,
I with my ink-stained
fingers that dig
and dig in air
for air. And I love
that black face
I have never seen
except in mirrors,
behind me, waiting
in the shadows.
I want to go down
into that mine
with my grandfather, each of us
with a single
clear eye
burning
at the front of our heads,
and put my hand
that I've kept clean
into his black one,
and let him show me
how the earth is a place
a man can go down into
every day
and make a living from,
even if it kills him.

The Elephant

I said it was an elephant's turd, but Fay, six, didn't be-
lieve me. She wanted to see for herself. I walked her
out to County 75, the gravel road a few blocks from

our house at the edge of town, where the thing lay, a gray and wrinkled dinner plate. Bending close to study it, she said, "I think it's tar." She had reason on her side, but I stuck to my story. At my age, I had had enough of reason, but she, at hers, was still coming into it. Nevertheless, I could tell that Fay wished she was wrong and I was right. She wanted that elephant turd to be there, in that most unlikely place. She wanted an elephant to have been walking near her house. She wanted to live in the kind of house near which, at any time, an elephant might walk. But her skeptical, rational self made her ask, "How did it get here?" I speculated that when the vans from the circus we had seen in Marshall the previous week drove past on the nearby highway, the back doors of the last one, the one containing the elephant, swung open—someone had forgotten to fasten them—and the elephant tumbled out, rolling surprised but unhurt into the ditch by the side of the road. We saw him then, if it was a him, after a minute or so push himself up and leave the highway to wander down the road leading into our town, a parade of firs on one side, a field of wheat on the other. It was night; the moon bathed his hide in milky light. We talked about how he'd feel, perhaps a little frightened, but glad, too, released from the truck, wandering at his own pace along the inviting gravel road and lifting his great head now and then to observe the domed and cloudless sky. We figured the stars would look to him like appreciative eyes shining through a darkened tent during one of his performances. This night's performance, however, would be his best because here he could act according to his own truest impulses. Tonight he took orders only from himself, listened only to internal cues. The wind was blowing, and he spread his ears out to catch more of it. The silky air must have said something to him about love as elephants know it. As he walked, he

swayed, and his tail waved behind him, shyly conduct-
ing the moon and the busy stalks of grain bent over
themselves like cellists. And then we saw him stop
and tense a little, just where we were standing, and
make himself even happier than he already was.

The Feet Man

for Leo Dangel

The worst job I ever had was nailing
Jesus' feet to the cross on the
assembly line at the crucifix factory.
Jesus! I'd never thought of myself
as religious before that, but when
I had to strike those nails—I figured
it up once—more than two thousand times
a day, my mind began seeing things:
little tremors along the skin, jerks of
those legs that were bonier than
models' legs, his eyes imploring,
forgiving. I swear, if a tiny drop of blood
had oozed out of that wood at my pounding,
I wouldn't have been surprised at all.
I was ripe for a miracle, or a vacation.
All I got was worse: with each blow
of the hammer, I flinched, as if I
were the one getting pierced. Doing
that job day after day was bad enough,
but doing it to myself—my arms
spread out from one end of my paycheck
to the other—was crazy. I began
to sweat constantly, though the place
was air-conditioned. It wasn't long before
the foreman took me aside and told me
I was taking my job too seriously, that

if I wanted to keep it I had better calm down.
He was right. I pulled myself together
like a man and put all pointless thoughts
out of my head. Or tried to. It wasn't easy:
imagine Jesus after Jesus coming down
at you along that line, and you with
your hammer poised, you knowing
what you have to do to make a living.

. . . .

C. G. HANZLICEK
(1942–)

C. G. Hanzlicek was born in Owatonna and educated at the University of Minnesota and the University of Iowa. From 1966 to 2001 he served as professor of English and director of the Creative Writing Program at California State University, Fresno. He is the author of eight volumes of poetry, including Stars *(winner of the Devins Award),* Calling the Dead, Mahler: Poems and Etchings, *and* The Cave: New and Selected Poems, *as well as two books of translations.*

The One Song

It's taken many years to find
He was right that evening long ago.
When the world you live in
Suddenly turns into a minefield,
And people at every step
Vanish in quick columns of smoke,
You begin to think death is the one song.
Now I know songs about the end
Ache in the throat
Only because love is there too.

I must have been five years old.
Black clouds were rolling across fields,
And there were flicks of lightning
On the horizon
Too distant for thunder,
But near enough to crackle the voice
Of a woman singing her heart out
In the little cathedral
Of the radio.

The song made my feet squirm;
I didn't know what to do with my hands,
So I put them in my pockets.
Why do they only sing about love,
Why always love?
He laughed to my mother,
Then looked at me very tenderly,
Like I was five
And a bit helpless in the head,
And gave me an honest answer:
What else is there to sing about?

Caretaking at the Bohemian Cemetery Outside Owatonna, Minnesota

One Saturday a gray squirrel
Led me past the carved names—
Ptacek, Novotny, Kubicek, Pelinka,
Risavy, Buryska, Hrdlicka,
Spatenka, Krahulec, Blazek, Wencl—
While my father and grandfather
Mowed and clipped around the tombstones.
Just where the cemetery
Ran into a green wall of corn,
I paused at a stone.
On its face was a glass oval,

And inside the oval
Was a portrait of a boy.
It was almost my own face,
But I was ten years old
And had outlived him by a year.
I looked so long at his eyes
I forgot about the squirrel,
And then I gathered pine cones
To lay upon his grave.
Now I've forgotten his name,
But I remember he died
In January of 1921.
The gravedigger must have cursed him
Silently for one full day,
Since a winter death
Meant dynamiting past the frostline
And lifting out heavy blocks of earth.
I stayed near him all afternoon—
I think I even prayed once for him—
Until I heard my father
Calling my name through the pines,
And all that evening
I stayed very near him.

. . . .

John Calvin Rezmerski
(1942–)

A native of Pennsylvania, John Calvin Rezmerski served for many years as writer-in-residence at Gustavus Adolphus College in St. Peter, Minnesota. In the 1970s, he led Minnesota Poetry Out Loud, taking groups of poets to perform poetry and music in small-town festivals, parks, churches, and senior centers. His work has earned the Devins Award, a National Endowment for the Arts Fellowship, and the Rhysling Award from the Science Fiction

Poetry Association. He is the author of Held for Questioning, An American Gallery, What Do I Know?: New & Selected Poems, *as well as the editor of* The Frederick Manfred Reader.

Willmar at Night

I have been to Willmar, Minnesota,
where the houses look pious.
At night they hear noises,
metal wheels squeaking and hissing,
the throb of engines biding their time.
The houses turn over in their sleep,
dreaming of following boxcars,
windows wide open, wind whupping
through parlors and bedrooms,
finally, in Fargo or St. Paul,
letting strangers enter
with whiskey and loud stereos.
I have been to Willmar, slept in Willmar,
crossed the tracks in Willmar at night.

Way Back

Sitting in a magic chair
composing my bible,
I begin
living backwards.
Moving toward my birth,
remembering less and less about death,
forgetting how to forget,
finally I am equal to anyone—
a drop of slippery water
in a velvet sack.
If you remember
reading this before,
you have not been unlearning your lessons.

You will not be saved.
Turn around and come with me
to the other end of our lives.

Growing Down

If you are ten years old
I am too late to tell you
what I would have told
all you nine-year-olds:
that at eight years old
you would have been better off
if you were still seven,
but not as well off
as if you were still six,
which is when things
start to go bad:
because you are not
five anymore and
have forgotten everything
you knew at four.
So you three-year-olds
are the ones I really
want to talk to,
because you remember
what it was like
to be two-and-a-half
when people were just
beginning to talk to you
for fun, but
not baby talk like
when you were two
and they treated you
like one-year-olds.
Anybody knows better
than to talk to a one-year-old.
They don't listen.

. . . .

MARK VINZ
(1942–)

Born in Rugby, North Dakota, Mark Vinz was raised in Minneapolis and the Kansas City area, and attended the universities of Kansas and New Mexico. A professor of English at Minnesota State University at Moorhead, he has played an instrumental role in the Minnesota literary community for decades. He founded Dacotah Territory, *one of the state's most successful literary journals in the 1970s, and served as editor of Territorial Press and Dacotah Territorial Press. He also cofounded Plains Distribution Service, a distributor for works by Midwestern writers and small independent presses. The recipient of a National Endowment for the Arts Fellowship, six Pen Syndicated Fiction Awards, and three Minnesota Book Awards, he is the author of many books, including* Long Distance, Late Night Calls, Climbing the Stairs, *and* Minnesota Gothic, *and has edited numerous others. He lives in Moorhead.*

Flat Country

after Dana Gioia

Give me a landscape where the sky is huge
with scudding, booming clouds—no walls of trees
obscuring hovering hawks, except along
the riverbanks where cottonwood and willow
watch meandering currents, ox-bowed in
their own stubborn time.
                    This is a place where
fences seem an afterthought, no mountains
to distract the eye from bluestem haze and
spikes of blazing star—spirit's reckoning
that rises with each plume of dust or smoke.

Perspective is the ground that creeps up from
the valley floor, reminding us of what
is coming from a long way off—rippling

the prairie grass, another universe
that spreads out all around us, at our feet.

Red River Blues

Tonight the news of drought
sweeps in on western winds—
topsoil laced with smoke and snow.
Nothing can stop that message here.

The empty rain gauge chants
the last faint summer dreams;
around the house the earth
has sunk another inch this week.

Even flat land falls away: this is
the place where all directions cease.
Just past town is the only hill—
the overpass for the Interstate.

Still Life with Thermometer

Today you remember windchill—
40, 50, 60 below—
after a point it ceases to matter.
Your car is sealed in ice.
All footprints have drifted over,
houses drawn up together
in a ring of smoke.

How do you speak of the real winter?
It's cold, you say. Cold.
It moves through doors and walls.
This is the way you have learned to speak,
without postmarks, without stamps.

You watch the dead growth
of last summer's garden
rising from the snow,
a spider frozen on the windowsill,
the gathering dark—
your own cloudy breath
bearing messages
to each corner of the room.

.   .   .   .

Tom Hennen
(1942–)

*Tom Hennen was born in Morris and grew up on farms in western Min-
nesota. He has worked as a laborer, migrant bean-picker, and stagehand, and
for many years he was employed by the Minnesota Department of Natural
Resources and the United States Fish and Wildlife Service. He is the author
of* Crawling Out the Window, Looking into the Weather, *and*
Love for Other Things: New and Selected Poems.

Out of Nothing

Snow began slowly. Only one flake fell all morning. It
was talked about by everyone as they gathered for
coffee. It brought back memories of other times.
Dreams of ice skates, long shotguns waving at geese,
cities lighting up somewhere off the prairie horizon
in the cold gray day. Only one snowflake but it fell
with the grace of a star out of the damp, ragged air. It
filled the day with a clarity seldom noticed. It stood
out sharply as a telephone pole against the skyline of
the winter we each keep to ourselves.

Crawling Out the Window

When water starts to run, winds come to the sky car-
rying parts of Canada, and the house is filled with the
scent of dead grass thawing. When spring comes on
the continental divide, the snowbanks are broken in
two and half fall south and half fall north. It's the Gulf
of Mexico or Hudson Bay, one or the other for the
snow, the dirt, the grass, the animals and me. The
Minnesota prairie has never heard of free will. It asks
you, quietly at first, to accept and even love your fate.
You find out that if you fall south, life will be easy, like
warm rain. You wake up with an outgoing personal-
ity and a knack for business. The river carries you.
You float easily and are a good swimmer. But if you
fall north while daydreaming, you never quite get
your footing back again. You will spend most of your
time looking toward yourself and see nothing but
holes. There will be gaps in your memory and you
won't be able to earn a living. You always point north
like a compass. You always have to travel on foot
against the wind. You always think things might get
better. You watch the geese and are sure you can fly.

. . . .

JOHN CADDY
(1937–)

*John Caddy is a third-generation native of the Mesabi Range in northeast-
ern Minnesota, and the descendant of Cornish hardrock miners. The recip-
ient of numerous awards, including fellowships from the Bush Foundation,
Minnesota State Arts Board, McKnight Foundation, and the Los Angeles
Times Book Prize, he helped found the Minnesota Poets-in-the Schools Pro-
gram. He has served as writer-in-residence at hundreds of schools through-*

out the state and has taught at Hamline University and the University of Minnesota. His collections of poetry include Eating the Sting *and* The Color of Mesabi Bones.

Mine Town: Knowing Where You're At

He saw nation in every cheekbone, every movement of a lip. Pops Schibel stood in front of Palace Clothing, greeting all in their mother tongues. Saw nation in a walk, the way a scarf or babushka was worn, and knew which of his seven tongues to greet. He apprenticed in Helsinki and Riga, Malmo and St. Petersburg, and in none of them could he own land.

Pops knew all these sons and daughters of hardrock miners who drilled underground in Budapest and Cornwall and Helsinki before they came across in the 1880s and 90s, jostling sons and daughters of the Canuck and Swede and Yank loggers who stayed to finish off the pine. Knew the steerage families from Italy and Montenegro, Finland and the Ukraine who came later with sharp elbows and notes on their clothes, knew the Greeks and Irish, the Baltic Jews, Chinese.

Nation was basic on the Mesabi. And where that tension ruled, so did clarity. A glaring clarity that let you know where you were at—like it or not. A restful clarity that saved the energy of *politesse*, saved work, allowed work. Clarity sired by Necessity out of Babel.

Here, even Italians said Eye-talian. To the rest, Dagos. Serb, Croatian, Slovanian—any Slav—lumped into Bohunk. Cornish were Cousin Jacks. Finns so lucid and sure they were simply *Suomilainens,* Finnlanders. Necessity: second and third-generation kids routinely insulted their friends to greet them, to defuse their parents' dislikes, their own suspicions. Insult with a smile. *Hey Dago, how ya doin?* Insult to enable love.

Years later in Anthropology 1A, I hear a lecture about the Eskimo custom of *joking relationships,* crude ritual insults to lower winter tensions and prevent murder. Norwegian and German farmboys furrow their brows and push forward heavily in their chairs, trying to comprehend, and for a change, I lean back and cross my feet, happy to hear of other civilized groups in the north, knowing where I'm at.

The War Effort

After supper I'd use the can opener to cut the bottoms off the day's tin cans, slip the two end circles inside the open cylinder, place them on the linoleum, and—freedom of noisy freedoms—stamp them flat. What could he say? They were for the War Effort. We were all Patriots. We had Drives: paper, scrap metal, old tires.

We carried dimes in our mittens to grade school to slowly buy Bonds. The teachers sold us small red stamps with the Concord Minuteman on them, and we'd lick them into books. A full book meant—the teachers always said it in full—a United States War Bond. We figured a jeep, maybe even a tank's worth.

We learned to talk in Capitals. We had Drives and Victory Gardens, Blackouts and Spies. Victory Gardens, I knew, had to make a "V" shape in the earth or they wouldn't help the war.

Spies were all around. The mines were Targets. Once
we saw a spy in a Piper Cub flying back and forth over
the pits. He used a heliograph only Scouts would no-
tice, sun flashing off the plane's windows. We wrote
each series of flashes down in Morse Code, but
couldn't cipher it. We showed it to a soldier home on
leave, but he couldn't break the code either.

Blackouts were best. Sirens would go off, house lights
blink yellow to black window by window. From the
front steps we watched night blot out the streetlights
block by block until the whole town was unmade.
We'd walk around the house with red cloth rubber-
banded over flashlights. Air raid wardens appeared
from the dark to inspect and complain about the guy
up the block who didn't pull his shades. We'd sit in
the living room and listen to the radio, kids dashing
to the window now and then to peel back curtains
and imagine searchlights tunneling the sky, hoping
for bombers, wondering if this would be the time, un-
til the All-Clear sounded. I learned something in
Blackouts. I didn't know what, but I knew it was big-
ger than our house. Think of it: a power so strong it
could make parents sit in the dark.

Mine Towns

Much abandoned now, forced out or grown over, gone,
thrown into memory's hole. You have to dig for it.
Water-filled pits, rusted washing plants and crushers.
Tracks and spurs that just stop. The white pine cut,
the iron dug out. Not even much red left. No dust
coating cars or ground into hands. But bones mix with ore
in these empty mines, and the bones are red.

Much has always died. Towns: old Mesaba, Adriatic, Elcor.
Old pavement weedsplit. Lost customs and recipes,
causes and countries. Words: *Poyka. Sisu.* Short old women
in black babushkas clumped in front of churches.
Sayings: *May the Devil carry you off in a sack!*
Whole languages: Serb, French, Italian, stubborn Finn,
merchants who could speak them.

Much has died. Some nourishes still. Strike dreams:
1907, the Wobblies in '16, the thirties, fifties—dreams
of a living wage, justice, victory. Lost homesteads and
     saunas,
Finnish dovetails still wedging the squared white pine,
Logging camps: a privy, a chimney half-standing.

Some refuses death: timewarp Friday nights
on Chestnut Street, bumper to cruising bumper, sidewalks
swirling, all the bars bright, everyone calling *Hey*
to everyone, the polka lilt to the voice and the eye.
Behind town, out in the woods in old jackpine slash,
polished cones grip their seeds like gray stones,
wait lifespans for the fire to bloom.

Much is buried for the digging. The Mill Forty:
tangled concrete roots of the world's largest sawmill.
Sprinkled through fields where the company
moved the houses off, open cellars choked with raspberries.
By the back steps, rhubarb still thrusts its spear,
comfrey sprawls, mints and lilies struggle with long grass.

Abandoned now, knocked down and forced out, thrown
into memory's hole, the shaft leading to the full heart
where it all and always is embraced and laugh-angry and
     alive.

. . . .

JILL BRECKENRIDGE
(1938–)

Originally from Boise, Idaho, Jill Breckenridge was educated at the University of Minnesota, Goddard College, and St. Mary's College in Winona, Minnesota. She is the author of How to Be Lucky *(winner of the Bluestem Award in Poetry) and* Civil Blood, *a book-length sequence of poetry and prose about the Civil War. She is the recipient of two Minnesota State Arts Board Fellowships, a Bush Foundation Fellowship, and the Loft-McKnight Writer's Award in both prose and poetry. A former director of the Loft Literary Center, she has taught in the Minnesota Writers-in-the-Schools Program and worked as a writing consultant, teaching workshops on business and technical writing.*

Beer Barrel Polka

Rising from the parking lot by Lake
Superior's beach, floating up between
red and gold leaves of birch and maple,
the accordion strains of Beer Barrel
Polka. How I hated practicing that song
until I got it right, hated strolling

among guests in my black taffeta skirt
and white satin blouse, playing Beer Barrel
Polka, the number I got the most requests
for, at my parents' drunken parties,

rooms hazed with cigarette smoke,
glasses in every hand; then Tea For Two,
the toothy gushing of women, scarlet
lipstick smeared across their teeth;
then Ghost Riders in the Sky, men's sly
looks, pinches, slack whiskey grins,

while I walked among them, a grim smile
pasted on my lips, as doomed as they
were, doing my time, serving my sentence
until I could make an escape, my right

hand stretched across the white keys,
my left hand pounding the bass notes,
as the bellows hissed, opened and closed,
opened and closed, and I, a snotty
little Cinderella, belted it out.

Now, from the beach, laughter echoes
up the hill with that jolly beer hall tune,
laughter mixed with blinding sunlight
and the sound of waves, as people pile out
of the car singing those stupid words, *Roll out
the barrel, we'll have a barrel of fun!*

and dance around the accordion player.
While gold and red leaves fall among them,
they shed for a moment their failures
and disappointments, as the accordion
squeezes a bit of delight from this cold

lemon of a world, and the awkward dancers,
tossed into a crazy circle by the song,
throw their heads back, wrap their arms
around each other, and reach for the reprieve

of laughter, stumble toward the fleeting
pardon of joy, just like my hapless parents
those many years ago, they and their drunken
friends long gone, all of us doomed, all
of us pardoned, all of us free at last.

Helen Hart's Summer Watercolor Class

She wore gold earrings
big as Kerr Jar lids,
and a purple scarf waving behind

her yellow jeep for blocks
as she picked us up for watercolor class.
She drove faster than our mothers'
voices calling us home.

Instead of aprons, she wore eyelashes
so long and black we couldn't
take our eyes off them. Her work
was our play, her play, our delight,

and her laugh sailed every pond
in Julie Davis Park, startling
the iridescent mallards
we girls painted, greens flowing
into blues, blues into greens.

Round-eyed, we stared up at gigantic
trees reaching over the still pond,
tried to take them in, couldn't keep them

on the page, leaves greening off
into blue's washed sky, trunks
dripping brown onto our bare toes.

It was the summer we wanted
to last beyond the white pages
of our artist pads,

until the next year when we discovered
boys and, blooming inside us, the roses
we'd only red-dotted on the page,

and lost our vision, stored our brushes
in metal tins, trees shrunk down to salt
and sugar, measured, then spooned
into nested silver bowls. We baked white
bread and brownies, timed everything,

nearly forgot where we'd hidden our colors—
the murmur of blue, red's rejoicing,
violet's tenor enhancing yellow's aria—

frozen squares of color, waiting for
the brush, a drop of water, background
light enough to let us through.

. . . .

BARTON SUTTER
(1949–)

*Born in Minneapolis, Barton Sutter grew up in rural towns in Minnesota
and Iowa, and was educated at Bemidji State University, Southwest State
University, and Syracuse University. His books include* Cedarhome,
Sequoyah, Pine Creek Parish Hall and Other Poems, The
Book of Names: New and Selected Poems, *and* Farewell to
the Starlight in Whiskey, *as well as books of fiction and nonfiction.
The recipient of numerous awards for his work, including three Minnesota
Book Awards, he lives in Duluth and teaches at the University of Wiscon-
sin, Superior.*

Sweet Jesus

I found you, my lush, curvaceous savior,
Nailed to the old rugged cross of your life
As if cursed, caught, condemned to stay there.

Sweet Jesus with breasts and black hair,
I took you down, dressed your wounds,
Woke you from your midlife swoon,
And made you my unlawful wife.
You drank the gall of my despair
But swore there was another way.
Our bodies would be the wine and bread
On which we fed. We came alive there,
Nourished by grief, by tears and saliva.
And, lo, the stone of sorrow was rolled away;
Together, we rose from the dead.

Whistle Dance

My grandmother from Hinckley told
My brother and me, when she'd grown old,
How they used to dance in farm country
Way back in the twentieth century.
"We'd go down through the woods with kerosene lanterns
To Andersons' barn, where we held our dances.
The way that light flashed off the birches,
Why, it was like candles in those Catholic churches.
The girls wore shawls, but we soon got warm.
Just a big bare room, and nothing more.
What did we care? We stomped up a storm.
Tom had a sweet harmonica. Or a fiddle played
Far into the night. We stayed and stayed.
Sometimes we didn't have anything!
We'd hold our darn dance anyway,
If all we could do was whistle and sing."

Swedish Lesson

Talk about the mother tongue.
I heard these words when I was young.

I'd gabble gibberish and stutter,
Mimicking my babysitters.
They'd say, "Can you speak svenska?"
I'd answer, "Ya, you betcha."
They'd giggle, slap their laps, and sigh.
Their gossip was my lullabye.
Around the barn their men would grunt
The Esperanto of immigrants.

My grandmother risked ridicule
Whenever she opened her mouth at school
But broke the brogue. I speak American,
But, feeling like a bad translation,
I bought the books and paid tuition.
My classmates mock my pronunciation.

Once these words were hawked and spit
By barbarians who meant it
When they swore. They drew swords
And mangled men for what they said.
These words are theirs but tamed by time,
Their history a wind chime.
Hearsay now, they sound so gentle
I think of women spinning wool.
Chuckling like a dandling song,
The melodic nonsense passes on
Rumors of the old country. We
Hear the schuss of snow and ski
Past places parents mentioned.
Strange. The teacher's intonation
Makes every other word a question.
Blue-collar misfits, dissatisfied
Housewives, we've stood beside
Our ancestors, laid hands on headstones,
Wondering why they ever left home,
Mystified by the rotten spoils
Of the Viking dream of silk and jewels.

We've traced the foreign, familiar names
Chiselled in grim cuneiform.
The rune stones resist interpretation.

And so we've begun this reverse migration.
God knows what we hope to learn.
The motives of the arctic tern?
We murmur, uncertain what we're about,
But, counting together, we launch the boat.
I swear by my grandmother's face
And steer to the north, northeast.
I stammer and repeat my faith
In the dead, their hope, their anguish,
Buried alive in this, their language.

. . . .

LOUIS JENKINS
(1942–)

Louis Jenkins was born and raised in Oklahoma and attended Wichita State University in Wichita, Kansas. His books of prose poems include An Almost Human Desire, Nice Fish: New and Selected Prose Poems, Just Above Water, *and* Sea Smoke. *During the 1970s, he coedited* Steelhead, *one of Minnesota's finest literary journals at the time. The recipient of numerous honors for his work, including two Bush Foundation Fellowships, the 1987 Loft-McKnight Award for Poetry, and a Minnesota Book Award, he lives in Duluth.*

Basketball

A huge summer afternoon with no sign of rain. . . .
Elm trees in the farmyard bend and creak in the
wind. The leaves are dry and gray. In the driveway a

boy shoots a basketball at a goal above the garage door. Wind makes shooting difficult and time after time he chases the loose ball. He shoots, re-bounds, turns, shoots . . . on into the afternoon. In the silence between the gusts of wind the only sounds are the thump of the ball on the ground and the rattle of the bare steel rim of the goal. The gate bangs in the wind, the dog in the yard yawns, stretches and goes back to sleep. A film of dust covers the water in the trough. Great clouds of dust rise from open fields that stretch a thousand miles beyond the horizon.

Mailboxes

Some are brightly painted and large as if anticipating great packages. Most are smaller, gray and dented with rust spots, some held together with rope or duct tape, having been slapped more than once by the snow plow. Still they seem hopeful . . . perhaps a Village Shopper or a credit card offer. . . . Once in a while one raises a modest tin flag. "I have something. It isn't much. I'd like you to take it." All along Highway 16, on Hunter Road and Dahl Road, past Cane Lake, past the gravel pit, and the last refrigerator shot full of holes and dumped into the swamp, mailboxes reach out on extended arms, all the way to the end of the route where balsam and spruce crowd together in the ditches, reaching out. . . .

Knife Island

From Stoney Point it appears as a green, rounded shape in Superior's waters, perhaps safe haven, the Promised Land, like the Lake Isle of Innisfree rising from the mist. Up close it's just a pile of rocks with a few stunted trees, a place beaten by water and wind, a squalor of seagulls. The whole place is covered with gulls, gull shit, feathers and broken eggs, gulls in the air, gulls on the water, gulls on the ground. It's a noisy place, threat and intimidation, outrage, and indignation, the constant squabbling over territory. Their cry, "Justice!" "You are in my space!" Seagulls, like humans, not comfortable alone, not happy together. This is life with all its horrible enthusiasm, better seen from a distance.

. . . .

BILL MEISSNER
(1948–)

Raised in Wisconsin and Iowa, Bill Meissner serves as Director of Creative Writing at St. Cloud University. He is the author of numerous books, including the poetry collections Twin Sons of Different Mirrors *(with Jack Driscoll),* The Sleepwalker's Son, Learning to Breathe Underwater, *and* American Compass, *as well as the collection of short stories* Hitting into the Wind. *Awards for his work include fellowships from the National Endowment for the Arts and Minnesota State Arts Board, two Loft-McKnight Awards, and five PEN/NEA Syndicated Fiction Awards. He lives in St. Cloud.*

First Ties: The Father in the Mirror

Fourteen, late for church, I stood in front of the mirror,
    fumbling
with the new tie until my father's face surfaced behind me.
Reaching in front of my chest, he led
the red and blue silk around and

under, under and
around in some mysterious
pattern. *Nothing to a tie,* he said.

For those few seconds, his big arms were my arms—
I watched the thick fingers
working the tie, each time a little
too short or too long.

He leaned his face alongside mine,
and I smelled a sharp scent of Old Spice, heard the hiss
   of sighs
through his nose, like a car tire losing air,
as he focused on the broad wrinkled pillar
that would not tie.
Arms that hadn't surrounded me for years
now wrapped me like ribbons. His elbows swung
like rhythmic pendulums, and
for an instant it looked like we could have been
dancing, so I stood still,
unable to pull away from the rough kiss of whiskers
against my smooth cheek.

He finally finished a crooked knot, slid it
up to my tender throat, too tight, too tight.
Just right, he said.
Then I understood
that being an adult meant
you looked a little older, but you couldn't breathe.
         I watched my father
         back away in the mirror and
         disappear, and all I could see was myself,
         the knot at my throat, a soft, angled
         embrace of cloth.

The Dance of the Ripples

The Saturday evening after Dad's funeral we find ourselves
    at the lake,
and Mom wades alone into the calm, darkening water.
Deep in grief, her skin is the color of silt. Concentric circles
move out from her thighs. The small ripples
hurry away from her, travel the distance
to the shore and reach us, her children,
who stand still, ankle-deep, unable to talk,
    the humid blanket
of dusk weighting down our shoulders.

At this lake tonight, everything
seems too quiet or too loud, rising or falling, moving or not
    moving.
One of us exhales with a soft hiss.

We watch her wade into deeper water, up to her waist,
    though
we all know she doesn't swim.
But it's her heart we worry about now, her small
red heart drowning inside the twilight of her body.
I want to call out to her:
Not so deep, not so deep. He's not here
to steady you when you step
into the drop-off.

Suddenly, music wafts through the screen of the pavilion:
Glenn Miller's saxophones roll smoothly toward us.
Mother faces the center of the lake.
Forgetting for a moment, she sways side to side to the
    rhythm,
sending out small sudden waves that glisten in the
    moonlight.
It seems as though someone should ask her to dance.

Then she closes her eyes, silencing the music
while the ripples clasp their rings
tightly around her waist,
holding her, holding her.

. . . .

ETHERIDGE KNIGHT
(1931–1991)

Born in Corinth, Mississippi, Etheridge Knight was the author of Poems
from Prison, *about his six years in the Indiana State Prison for armed
robbery,* Belly Song and Other Poems, *and* The Essential Ether-
idge Knight. *He was the recipient of the National Book Award in Poetry
and fellowships from the Guggenheim Foundation and the National Endow-
ment for the Arts, and in 1985 was awarded the Shelley Memorial Award by
the Poetry Society of America in recognition of distinguished achievement
in poetry. He lived in Minnesota in the 1970s and conducted workshops in
the Twin Cities.*

Hard Rock Returns to Prison from the Hospital for the Criminal Insane

Hard Rock / was / "known not to take no shit
From nobody," and he had the scars to prove it:
Split purple lips, lumbed ears, welts above
His yellow eyes, and one long scar that cut
Across his temple and plowed through a thick
Canopy of kinky hair.

The WORD / was / that Hard Rock wasn't a mean nigger
Anymore, that the doctors had bored a hole in his head,
Cut out part of his brain, and shot electricity

Through the rest. When they brought Hard Rock back,
Handcuffed and chained, he was turned loose,
Like a freshly gelded stallion, to try his new status.
And we all waited and watched, like a herd of sheep,
To see if the WORD was true.

As we waited we wrapped ourselves in the cloak
Of his exploits: "Man, the last time, it took eight
Screws to put him in the Hole." "Yeah, remember when he
Smacked the captain with his dinner tray?" "He set
The record for time in the Hole—67 straight days!"
"Ol Hard Rock! man, that's one crazy nigger."
And then the jewel of a myth that Hard Rock had once bit
A screw on the thumb and poisoned him with syphilitic spit.

The testing came, to see if Hard Rock was really tame.
A hillbilly called him a black son of a bitch
And didn't lose his teeth, a screw who knew Hard Rock
From before shook him down and barked in his face.
And Hard Rock did *nothing.* Just grinned and looked silly,
His eyes empty like knot holes in a fence.

The Idea of Ancestry

1
Taped to the wall of my cell are 47 pictures: 47 black
faces: my father, mother, grandmothers (1 dead), grand-
fathers (both dead), brothers, sisters, uncles, aunts,
cousins (1st & 2nd), nieces, and nephews. They stare
across the space at me sprawling on my bunk. I know
their dark eyes, they know mine. I know their style,
they know mine. I am all of them, they are all of me;
they are farmers, I am a thief, I am me, they are thee.

I have at one time or another been in love with my mother,
1 grandmother, 2 sisters, 2 aunts (1 went to the asylum),

and 5 cousins. I am now in love with a 7-yr-old niece
(she sends me letters written in large block print, and
her picture is the only one that smiles at me).

I have the same name as 1 grandfather, 3 cousins, 3 nephews,
and 1 uncle. The uncle disappeared when he was 15, just took
off and caught a freight (they say). He's discussed each year
when the family has a reunion, he causes uneasiness in
the clan, he is an empty space. My father's mother, who is 93
and who keeps the Family Bible with everybody's birth dates
(and death dates) in it, always mentions him. There is no
place in her Bible for "whereabouts unknown."

2
Each fall the graves of my grandfathers call me, the brown
hills and red gullies of mississippi send out their electric
messages, galvanizing my genes. Last yr / like a salmon
    quitting
the cold ocean-leaping and bucking up his birthstream / I
hitchhiked my way from LA with 16 caps in my pocket and a
monkey on my back. And I almost kicked it with the
    kinfolks.
I walked barefooted in my grandmother's backyard / I
    smelled the old
land and the woods / I sipped cornwhiskey from fruit jars
    with the men /
I flirted with the women / I had a ball till the caps ran out
and my habit came down. That night I looked at my
    grandmother
and split / my guts were screaming for junk / but I was
    almost
contented / I had almost caught up with me.
(The next day in Memphis I cracked a croaker's crib
    for a fix.)

This yr there is a gray stone wall damming my stream, and
    when

the falling leaves stir my genes, I pace my cell or flop on my
　　bunk
and stare at 47 black faces across the space. I am all of them,
they are all of me, I am me, they are thee, and I have no
　　children
to float in the space between.

.　.　.　.

MICHAEL DENNIS BROWNE
(1940–)

*Born in England, Michael Dennis Browne came to the United States in
1965. A graduate of the Creative Writing Program at the University of
Iowa, he has taught at Iowa, Columbia, Bennington, and, since 1971, the
University of Minnesota, where he is professor of English and former direc-
tor of the Creative Writing Program. He has received fellowships from the
National Endowment for the Arts, the Bush Foundation, and the Jerome
Foundation. His awards include Discovery 1968, The Borestone Prize, a
Loft-McKnight Award, and two Minnesota Book Awards. His many books
include* The Wife of Winter, You Won't Remember This, Se-
lected Poems, *and* Things I Can't Tell You.

Company of Love

Into the company of love / it all returns
Robert Creeley

Who do you carry? Who goes with you?
Who is there in the dark? In the night sweats?
Who will be there with you in the fire?
Who the companions? Are they not starlight?
How many songs have there been? Do you not hold those
　　tunes?
How many roadside flowers? How many summer fires?

Who is it bends over you again at night to kiss you?
Who do *you* bend to kiss? Whose laughs, whose tears are
  those?
Who lives on in your voice or do they not do that?
Who are the lanterns? Who have you there in the dark?
Who is near and very near? Is there not treasure?
Is there not blessing? Is everything buried to stay there?
Whose dreams can be there in yours? Who can you feed?
Who do you carry with you? Who goes along?

To Show Peter the World

Are we, perhaps, here just for saying:
house, bridge, well, gate, jug, fruit-tree, window . . .
R. M. Rilke (Ninth Duino Elegy)

It seems as if sometimes in sleep
the names drift off from their things.
The name-mist lifts. The things shine, clean.
On other nights the usual heavens
slide under and are gone.
New constellations gleam, suggestive.

It seems that I am bound to be
yet one more Adam, with my seven-month son;
not Lear, exhausted, bearing his daughter
at the very end of things, vowing
with all music what can never be, but
at the beginning, Peter, in truth
at the start of it all. *We two will sing.*

There are days, child, I have woken
ashamed of the names, wanting,
for your entering, fresher ones
for what you will come to know,
and what I must learn to do, all

over again, is trust the necessity,
the endlessness, the grace of our naming,
which is human, which is what we do,
and sound again around lips and teeth and tongue,
and roll again down bones and veins,
familiar syllables, yes, the usual ones,
until they assume the unknown again,
until no name's familiar, and learn

not only to wander with you
the present borders of our naming
but to be there to watch and listen
as you begin going on beyond,
making *your* names for the things, as
Peter shows Peter the world, this place
into which we have only brought you,
and in which we must leave you.

Handicapped Children Swimming

for Lamar

A measure of freedom. Mike, floating,
would not manage so without
the red life-jacket but would sink,

messy as weed; but with it
lies, weak, like a shirt,
and the eyes, and the tongue

uncontrolled, extended, show
the delight it is to be
horizontal on water, strapped there

by nothing but sunlight. Connie,
who otherwise moves with crutches
and stiff braces, is strong

through water. Becky, seeing always
badly, lies washed by the sense
of her own fragility, liking

the help of warm hands. Gregg
rides and plucks at the water
while Danny makes his own music

in his mind as he lilts
completely quiet. Mike's delight
opens like a flower as he floats.

He doesn't know he is floating
now in this poem. I have
nothing in fact to sustain him

and I know he will never stand
up alone. But whatever sustains
the children here is important;

Inflamed with the success
of water, released, they mingle
and soften there, as wax

on wetness, limp as wet bread
on water's kindness. Those fingers
can grasp as competently at air

and water as mine. Their bodies
are milky and do not need
cleansing, except from deformity.

Water cannot wash their
awkwardness from them, water is
simple, and defects difficult;

but they ride for a while, never
as free as the times they fly
in dreams, over the cliffs

harvesting in the sea, the bats
exquisite with radar, but
something, a measure of freedom.

And Mike is lucid on water,
still physically cryptic, physically
glinting, but Mike has grace

for a while, this is his best
floating since before birth,
where he lay bunched like any

other unformed—encircled, contained,
his mother not knowing the
uncontrol of those limbs that

threshed and kicked at her
from out of the orchard of water.
Light strolls among them, padding

healthy, firm, as these imperfect
children perch rolling in the foliage
of water, shifting to new flowerings

of face, though their limbs are
weeds. The shock comes when you see
the muscular men who played

with them in the pool carry them
in huddles from the pool, sunlight
spreading its crime on them.

.   .   .   .

CARY WATERMAN
(1942–)

Cary Waterman was born in Connecticut and educated at the University of Denver and Minnesota State University at Mankato. Among her many honors are two Minnesota State Arts Board Fellowships, two Bush Foundation Fellowships, a Tyrone Guthrie Fellowship, and the Loft-McKnight Poetry of Distinction Award. She has taught at Augsburg College, Metropolitan State University, the Loft Literary Center, and the Minneapolis College of Art and Design. She is the author of When I Looked Back You Were Gone, Dark Lights the Tiger's Tail, *and* The Salamander Migration and Other Poems, *and coeditor with Jim Moore of* Minnesota Writes: Poetry. *She lives in St. Paul.*

Crocus

One crocus in bloom suddenly.
I find it on the shelf beside
my bed with its sprawled sheets
and the empty clothes left
breathless on the floor.
This flower of resurrection,
forced through the hard soil of a pot,
has come stabbing into air.
It is purple and gloved
like many hands, one folded
on the other, covering the secret
night birth, the sound of quick breaths
not able to be held.

Now it is here,
first flower of spring
which you have given to me.
And how easy it is to wait
for the rest, accepting
the shortness of this life

which is persistent,
to be counted on,
like the sun that comes this morning
filtered through white curtains
that separate, but only slightly,
what is in the body
and what is not.

Visiting the Mayo Clinic

*Both clothes (the outer garment of the body) and illness (a kind of interior
décor of the body) became tropes for new attitudes toward the self.*
Susan Sontag, *Illness as Metaphor*

Suffering laps the edges of this town
like a lake that has been diseased
for many years.
But nearly everyone is
impeccably dressed,
everyone neat, new-pressed,
showing no frailty in the elevators,
keeping whatever it is that crouches
inside the body locked up.

There are only a few
who break through their disguises.
A woman in the lobby,
her hands spread in front of her
like pink fish encased
in a clear plastic bag.
And a few old men,
nervous in their suits
beside their suntanned, healthy wives.

Still how gracefully we all fold ourselves
like water lilies

into the chairs placed for waiting.
How easily the petals of our breathing
rise and fall.

And now I want to sleep.
I want to close my eyes on it,
finger the antique bone that is in my jaw,
and dream only of the next appointment.

.   .   .   .

JIM MOORE
(1943–)

*Jim Moore was born and raised in Decatur, Illinois, and was educated at
Carleton College, the University of Minnesota, and the University of Iowa.
He has taught at the Minneapolis College of Art and Design, the University
of Minnesota, Hamline University, and Colorado College. The recipient of
many awards and honors for his work, including three Minnesota Book
Awards and fellowships from the Bush Foundation, McKnight Foundation,
and the Minnesota State Arts Board, he is the author of six poetry collections,
among them* The Freedom of History, The Long Experience of
Love, *and* Lightning at Dinner, *and coeditor with Cary Waterman of*
Minnesota Writes: Poetry. *He lives in St. Paul.*

Near Herons

1
With the sun a full inch above the horizon, comes
the wind. The old man, becalmed in a white shirt, stands
with hands in pockets before the world's freshening,
the water in the bay beginning to shrug and shiver under the
     spur
of the raw, still unsettled light. Think of them, old men

all over the world sliding on their shoes in the dark,
by feel alone. Old men who do not wake their wives,
but step quietly out on the grass or sand
and stand in a place where they can see the sun
rejoin the world once again.

2
It is my pleasure to think of the men: my need
to see them facing open water near herons,
ordering nothing to happen
in these, the last days of their lives.
Near herons who know how to leave earth for miles
at a time. Creatures who, when stirred, open their wings
without a sound and lift themselves into another world.

What the Bird Sees

You rise up in the darkness,
over my body.
The white necklace at your throat,
the balls of ivory around your neck.
You open
your water-lily flesh
high up the side of the mountain in its own pond,
swaying, unafraid.
The blossoms rise small and tight
out of the green lips of the palmy leaves.

Need has found its breasts and entered them.
You invite me;
the leaves of your blooming are wide and wet.

The motionless bird on the chimney flies up.
It saw something there in the distance,
maybe another blackness like itself,

maybe the soft curl of sticks and hay woven in the circle
    of a nest.
The weave of darkness, the ivory beads, the sticks and hay
of our mingling breaths. We saw what the bird sees
and bore up our separate wings to that waiting nest.

I Don't Think We Need to Know

I don't believe we need to know what below zero feels like.
Or why we die: that, too, I don't think we need to know.
Why life is hard? I think not.

It's hot inside, it's cold out:
that's already a lot to know. That love comes and goes,
that we grow old slowly and then suddenly not.

It helps to know that snow is a god fallen to earth.
Sometimes it helps to let in the world a bit:
some wind, a few flakes, the sound of ice cracking.

Stars, for reasons we'll never know, help show us
who on earth we are and how to bear it here and how
far away we are from knowing why we are small.

Who knows why we love or why we die,
or what exactly wonder is,
demanding that I touch it as if it were the beloved

and I the young bride, believing.

.   .   .   .

P A T R I C I A H A M P L
(1946–)

A resident of St. Paul, Patricia Hampl is the author of A Romantic Education, I Could Tell You Stories: Sojourns in the Land of Memory, Woman Before an Aquarium, Resort and Other Poems, *and* Blue Arabesque, *among others. She has also edited or co-edited* Burning Bright: An Anthology of Sacred Poetry, The Houghton Mifflin Anthology of Short Fiction, *and* The Saint Paul Stories of F. Scott Fitzgerald. *The recipient of fellowships from the Guggenheim Foundation, Bush Foundation (twice), National Endowment for the Arts (twice), Ingram Merrill Foundation, and MacArthur Foundation, she serves as Regents' Professor and McKnight Distinguished Professor at the University of Minnesota, where she teaches in the Master of Fine Arts Program of the English department.*

Mother-Daughter Dance

Because it is late
because we fought today
because it was hot
and heat is an excuse
to be alone,
I sit in this chair stuffed
with old sun, leftover heat.

Our fight. The subject as always was history.
You made me look over my shoulder.
Mother was back there, speaking
to us in epilepsy, that language
she learned on her own,
the one we encouraged her to use
at the dinner table.
In my mind, I fell down, writhing,
trying to make history repeat itself,
burning with translations of guilt

for the men in the family.
Father forced a yellow pencil
between Mother's teeth, like a rose:
you die if you swallow your tongue.

All afternoon you yelled at me
as I slithered nearer to her.
We were doing the mother-daughter sweat dance,
salt dance, sexy Spanish rose dance.
You were yelling from the English language,
that fringed island I swim toward at night.
"The pencil," you were screaming in your language,
"Take the pencil from her mouth.
Write it down,
write your message down."

Woman Before an Aquarium

The goldfish ticks silently,
little finned gold watch
on its chain of water,
swaying over the rivulets of the brain,
over the hard rocks and spiney shells.

The world is round, distorted
the clerk said when I insisted
on a round fishbowl.
Now, like a Matisse woman,
I study my lesson slowly,
crushing a warm pinecone
in my hand, releasing
the resin, its memory of wild nights,
my Indian back crushing
the pine needles, the trapper
standing over me, his white-dead skin.

Fear of the crushing,
fear of the human smell.
A Matisse woman always wants
to be a mermaid,
her odalisque body
stretches pale and heavy
before her and the exotic wall hangings;
the only power of the woman:
to be untouchable.

But dressed, a simple Western face,
a schoolgirl's haircut, the plain desk
of ordinary work, she sits
crushing the pinecone of fear,
not knowing it is fear.
The paper before her is blank.
The aquarium sits like a lantern,
a green inner light, round
and green, a souvenir
from the underworld,
its gold residents opening and closing
their wordless mouths.

I am on the shore of the room,
glinting inside
with the flicker of water,
heart ticking with the message
of biology to a kindred species.
The mermaid—not the enchantress,
but the mermaid of double life—
sits on the rock, combing
the golden strands of human hair,
thinking as always
of swimming.

The Moment

Standing by the parking-ramp elevator
a week ago, sunk, stupid with sadness.
Black slush puddle on the cement floor,
the place painted a killer-pastel
as in an asylum.
A numeral 1, big as a person,
was stenciled on the cinder block:
Remember your level.
The toneless bell sounded.
Doors opened, nobody inside.
Then, who knows why, a rod of light
at the base of my skull flashed
to every outpost of my far-flung body—
I've got my life back.
It was nothing, just a present moment
occurring for the first time in months.
My head translated light,
my eyes spiked with tears.
The awful green walls, I could have stroked them.
The dirt, the moving cube I stepped into—
it was all beautiful,
everything that took me up.

.   .   .   .

JOHN MINCZESKI
(1947–)

A native of South Bend, Indiana, John Minczeski has taught at Macalester College, St. Cloud State University, and the University of Minnesota. A graduate of the Master of Fine Arts Program in Creative Writing at Warren Wilson College, he is the author of The Reconstruction of Light, Gravity, *and* Circle Routes *(winner of the Akron Poetry Prize), and*

editor of Concert in Chopin's House: A Collection of Polish-
American Writing. *Other honors include fellowships from the National
Endowment for the Arts and the Bush Foundation and a Loft-McKnight
Award in Poetry. He lives in St. Paul.*

Note to Trish from the Flamingo Motel, Long Prairie, Minnesota

for Patricia Hampl

Last time I was here the *Challenger* exploded
across America—the boosters' white plumes
twisting until it looked oddly beautiful
against the sky's dark blue. Now,
the week after Thanksgiving, Christmas lights

blossom on trees, outline entire houses
in flashing color. The guy who had a coronary last week
is bolting a sleigh to his roof. On Tuesday, my guide
pointed out the toy collector's house, a maroon
and cream Schwinn in his picture window,
as though Christmas had arrived early;
the corner where all summer a man waves
at passing cars; the house of the child molester
who had to leave his clothes behind

when they hauled him to jail. High school kids
drive back from the dance hall in Browerville
through the roll call of alcohol. Some work
graveyard shift at the packing plant and sleep
through morning classes. Long Prairie, Minnesota.
From the hills, it looks like a postage stamp,
and I could see myself here, so help me,
greasing my skin to keep from cracking,
loading logs into the fire nights like this,
and hunkering down like the cold itself
released at last from the driving wind.

Thaw

It is mire and muck down to the frost line,
all melt through the flooded fields;
an intermittent sky, encroaching woods
as I drive; every dip in the road's another culvert
through which the spring thaw shoots mud and sky
just this side of ice
swollen out of the muscles of snow
as the run-off grinds through sandstone,
more diamond than water.

At Pine City the river deserves its name
Snake, except it roars instead of rattles
as it twists and rolls like fire
drawing a million sirens towards its smoke
and calls a two-year-old who waits
until his mother's back is turned.
Three weeks later the river's tame again.
The parents stand outside their cabin
saying to reporters *he's gone back,*
he's just gone back. The newsmen
pause, the camera augurs in.

The men in hip boots have given up dragging
and gone to hand-tied flies. How deaf I am, driving past
that moment the river wailed,
stampede bulging in the middle, tearing out
trees and banks, gnawing itself and craving
anything this once besides itself,
anybody's child.

Excelsior Amusement Park, 1932

Captain Jack Payne, thick as a bulldog,
isn't smiling atop the hundred-foot ladder—

it's the Depression, after all. He licks
a finger to the wind and waits, ready
to lean forward, a jackknife
slicing through blazing water.

A loaf of bread only costs a nickel,
but the show's free, bless you, sirs.
Of course, the tank's deeper
than five feet—Captain Jack's no fool—
and he only climbs eighty rungs.
What the rubes don't know won't hurt.

The crowd presses against the ropes
to watch him fall according to the formula
Galileo calculated when everything
—souls and thought—was supposed to rise.
Captain Jack stands, shoulders squared,
on a swaying plank in the sky,

in the infinity of wind, solid American
syllables blaring from the loudspeaker:
Whenever you're ready, Captain!
Pressing against the ladder, he waits
for the final metallic words to reach him:
And good luck on your downward *journey.*

. . . .

MARILYN NELSON
(1946–)

Marilyn Nelson was born in Cleveland, Ohio, and educated at the University of California–Davis, the University of Pennsylvania, and the University of Minnesota. She is the author of For the Body, Mama's Promises, The Fields of Praise: New and Selected Poems, *and*

A Wreath for Emmett Till. *Her honors include two fellowships from the National Endowment for the Arts, the PEN/Winship Prize, a Guggenheim Fellowship, and the Newbery Award. She serves as emeritus professor of English at the University of Connecticut, Poet Laureate of Connecticut, and founder of Soul Mountain Retreat, a writer's colony. She taught at St. Olaf College from 1972 to 1978.*

Minor Miracle

Which reminds me of another knock-on-wood
memory. I was cycling with a male friend,
through a small midwestern town. We came to a 4-way
stop and stopped, chatting. As we started again,
a rusty old pick-up truck, ignoring the stop sign,
hurricaned past scant inches from our front wheels.
My partner called, "Hey, that was a 4-way stop!"
The truck driver, stringy blond hair a long fringe
under his brand-name beer cap, looked back and yelled,
    "You fucking niggers!"
And sped off.
My friend and I looked at each other and shook our heads.
We remounted our bikes and headed out of town.
We were pedaling through a clear blue afternoon
between two fields of almost-ripened wheat
bordered by cornflowers and Queen Anne's lace
when we heard an unmuffled motor, a honk-honking.
We stopped, closed ranks, made fists.
It was the same truck. It pulled over.
A tall, very much in shape young white guy slid out:
greasy jeans, homemade finger tattoos, probably
a Marine Corps boot-camp footlockerful
of martial arts techniques.

"What did you say back there!" he shouted.
My friend said, "I said it was a 4-way stop.
You went through it."

"And what did I say?" the white guy asked.
"You said: 'You fucking niggers.'"
 The afternoon froze.

"Well," said the white guy,
 shoving his hands into his pockets
 and pushing dirt around with the pointed toe of his boot,
"I just want to say I'm sorry."
 He climbed back into his truck
 and drove away.

. . . .

Deborah Keenan
(1950–)

Born in Minneapolis, Deborah Keenan has served in the Minnesota Poets-in-the-Schools Program and as managing editor of Milkweed Editions, and has taught at the Loft Literary Center as well as at the universities of St. Thomas, Hamline, and Minnesota. The recipient of a National Endowment for the Arts Fellowship, two Bush Foundation Fellowships, a Minnesota State Arts Board Fellowship, and the Loft-McKnight Poetry of Distinction Award, she is the author of six volumes of poetry, including The Only Window That Counts, Happiness, Good Heart, *and* Willow Room/Green Door. *She is also the coeditor of* Looking for Home: Women Writing About Exile, *which received the 1991 American Book Award.*

The Amateur

Whenever a celebrated murder occurred Bolden was there at the scene drawing amateur maps. There were his dreams of his children dying. There were his dreams of his children dying. There were his dreams of his children dying.

Coming Through Slaughter, Michael Ondaatje

In seventh grade geography we colored maps.
The continent of Africa was assigned when I
was in my red period. Each exotic country
challenged my crayons, my sense of harmony.
Cardinal red, plum, violet for the African
flowers on my mother's window ledge, wine,
the dark continent blossomed under my
steady left hand. Never before have so
many stars risen at the top of my work.
A true amateur, I colored for love.

An amateur parent at twenty-one, I was in
my blue period, to match my son's eyes and
the heaviness in my heart. His infant kabuki
hands defined the air, my dreams grew unsteady
as he grew more beautiful. I charted elaborate
plans for my life without him, while he dreamt
of clowns coming through the window to scratch
his eyes, and so we painted clowns, coloring
in details of anonymous faces, red stars on
flat white cheeks, blue triangles over empty
eyes. He slept easier then, while I dreamt
of masked men pushing him through the bedroom
window after disconnecting the stereo, severing
the telephone cord.

When my daughter in her dark beauty arrived,
I longed for hours of dream-filled sleep,
but she upset the mapping out I did for her
future with illness, her unsteady breathing
became the rhythm of my nights, for a year
all nights were broken, and she and I did
the rocking chair dance and far away in Africa
civil wars changed the names of half the countries
I had colored, believing they would never be altered.

It doesn't matter how many scientists explore
the country of sleep. It doesn't matter that

police draw white chalk lines around bodies
violently dispatched to eternity. Nothing
defines absence, there are no colors to choose
from when drawing in the shapes of missing
children, and when they slip away as you hold them,
or disappear under car wheels, or swim too far
in your dreams of water there are no rescues
plotted, the god of dreams is malevolent,
a professional, and you have done it all
for love, the competition is fixed, and the dream
of death is the first blossom after a child
blooms under your skin.

Dialogue

I ask my mother to remember
the tennis courts   nets always
too high or sagging like old ones in the park

I asked my father about the sun
breaking on our backs as we struggled
to bring order to the wild raspberry patch

I asked a stranger on a country street
about Orion's belt   about his dagger
about winter's secret constellations

I asked my lover to notice the light
how it fills all second story windows   fills steeples
fills the white car at quarter to five in a winter afternoon

my mother takes that single memory
turns it to a recital of my childhood
clarified through the sieve of her watching eyes

my father   gone now and cold
answered   keep working
summer is brief here

the stranger said only that he liked stars
too shy to say more
an innocent in a world of dark

my lover listened said the light was Italian
had traveled here from Florence   said the light
was correct   that twilight was good
said he would not leave in twilight in winter in that light

there have been questions
I never knew there were answers to

there have been so many answers
they have all been right

None of This

If it hadn't been for the cup of cold coffee
None of this would have happened. I wouldn't
Have walked away from my work, I wouldn't have
Opened the back door and let myself out into the world.

What we wanted from the garden this year was simple.
First, we wanted the dirt to look good. The weeds,
Dandelions, creeping charlie had to go.

Then we wanted food so we planted vegetables.
We turned to the small messages on the seed packets.
We did the work.

Now the garden is full, and it doesn't take a prophet
To know it will be bountiful; the vegetables are dependable,
We remember to water.

Then the coffee. That was, I guess, the postmodern
Moment in an old-fashioned life. The last thing we wanted

Was beauty, but I stepped into the garden and thought
About color, I thought about time and usefulness and
Beauty all at the same time and the birds lifted
And left me alone.

And now one of us might say perennial reds. One of us
Might talk about cosmos, one of us might be sick with
Longing for hollyhocks or the peace rose, and one of
Us might say annuals don't keep us up at night
Worrying about death.

.   .   .   .

JOHN ENGMAN
(1949–1996)

*John Engman was educated at Augsburg College and the University of Iowa.
He was the recipient of numerous awards for his work, including a Min-
nesota State Arts Board Fellowship, a Loft-McKnight Writers Award, a
Bush Foundation Fellowship, and the Helen Bullis Prize in Poetry from
Poetry Northwest. He taught in the writing programs at the University
of Minnesota, St. Olaf College, and the Loft Literary Center, and was the
author of* Alcatraz, Keeping Still, Mountain, *and* Temporary
Help.

Creation of the Universe

A tired angel
lugs a battered horn
up the steps of the cloud tower
but must rest on the escarpment

before awakening the sleepy molecules
with three weak blasts—for all I know,

it was like that.
Then Julia steps from number six,
on her way to the store for cigarettes,
and John crawls underneath his Rambler
to install new gaskets while David,
who hasn't yet suffered a cardiac,

tinkers with his ham radio,
still alive in number five.
Is Roger playing canasta in the basement?
Linda is up to her elbows in suds,
wondering if creatures live in outerspace
and what such creatures think of her,
who spends so much of an early evening
washing socks in the bathroom sink?
Rochelle and her guy have finally found heaven
and can't even hear the flutophone music
dripping like tears from number seven.
Anita roams the halls on rollerblades.
Greg has not arrived with three mad cats!
Margaret, gone uptown, and the evening calm:
I sit at my desk, as usual, writing a poem
as if working a puzzle, working a psalm . . .

Grace, in the kitchen of number three,
fans her stove with the old green rag
she wears in winter to keep the cold
away when she stays up late to talk
with friends who've gone before her to grave,
and watch the stars on Johnny Carson.
Her dinner of franks and red potatoes
has caught fire again, and her smoke alarm
can just be heard through the walls,
shrill and sweet as the lovesick
call of the cicada . . .

An Elephant

I abandoned Sharon first.
Sharon claims she abandoned me.
The dog abandoned both of us,
and wherever he went, stays put.
It's awfully hard to talk about,
but I still love her, madly.
In my dreams, or so she says,
she pats the dog. Maybe the dog
dreams we're together again,
sitting around admiring the dog.

His name was Shep.
Although I often called him
Sharon when I was adrift
on the barren island of desire,
where even Sharon could have been
good company, the Sharon I left,
who often called me Shep.
Although she would never admit
what she said, she will admit
she can't remember what she said,
and that was the whole problem
with our relationship: Shep.
The dog was our family secret.
Me, calling Shep by Sharon,
and Sharon, calling me by Shep.
It's awfully hard to talk about,
but the day I left, the day before
Sharon claims that she left me,
Shep called it quits and left us.
No one can build a relationship
on just the memory of a dog.

Sharon says she loved me
but the dog came between us.

Then she says, turns around
and says, we were never in love,
but that she still loves Shep.
I love tragedy as much as anyone,
but not being in one with a dog.
Sharon, you know I will never forget,
and someday I hope that you
will remember all three of us, fondly.
Shep, you know I will never forget
those nights you sat by the bed,
making eyes at us while we made love.
And Shep will never forget us, I know.
That dog had a memory like an elephant.

Chlorine

In the shallow end,
where I can stand,
I let the water

chill me slowly,
pull on skull cap
and plastic goggles.

I check my pulse.
Then do laps,
one lap for each year

of my life on earth,
a long mile back
to the year of my birth.

I swim by the house
where I grew up.
I swim by my father

and mother and sister
and gramps. The little
blonde boy who waves

is me. At the deep end,
I flip and turn back,
circle like a thought

through the overbearing
blue that children use
to portray the sky.

Then nothing left of me
but blue and the smell
of chlorine, flowers

plucked from the tomb
of an ancient King
who died young.

.　.　.　.

MARY KARR
(1955–)

Born in Groves, Texas, Mary Karr is the author of Viper Rum, The
Devil's Tour, Abacus, The Liar's Club, *and* Sinners Welcome.
She is the recipient of a Bunting Fellowship from Radcliffe College, a Whiting Writers Award, two Pushcart Prizes (in poetry and essay), and the Tietjens Award from Poetry Magazine. *Other honors include fellowships from the National Endowment for the Arts and the Minnesota State Arts Board, as well as the International Poetry Forum's Charity Randall Citation for Poetry and the PEN/Martha Albrand Award. A graduate of Macalester College, she has taught poetry and literature at Tufts, Harvard, Sarah Lawrence, and Syracuse University.*

The Pallbearer

for John Engman

The coffin I bore swung between us
like a battering ram against the door to heaven.
My friend was heavy carried by handles.

I listed. The plod was slow (no dirge).
The cherrywood cover got pittered with rain,
glossy with swirls in the grain

as with great red rivers risen to flood.
I too was flooded. My eyes brimmed
the green world blurry, though my face stayed flat.

The rhythm of walking took all my thought.
Later the shovels of dirt fell splat
on that cover, and they left a nice mound

like the start of a rose garden.
When I stretched on my narrow bed that night
I almost felt the strong hands heave me up;

my body swung through the dark like a child's.

The Worm-Farmer's Lament

If you git work, write,
That's what they shouted after your great
and not-so great whomevers,
who trudged away down wagon ruts walking
so as not to piss off the mule, away
from Bumfuck, Georgia, Flathead, Tennessee,
the iron skillets strapped to their backs
receding into dots on the map,

while those remaining took up
pickaxes or lit candles
over their foreheads then descended
to various infernos.
                              The travelers had it no better:
bandits slit their throats; their oxen
fell sick and slobbered; their babies' faces
were masked in lengths of calico
they'd scrimped to buy.

And still, they bore it,
being washed forward like so much
gorgeous debris, ferried by will
and the dumb hope that by grunting up
the next hill, one could reach a clearing
gold with sunflowers and there
burdens could be unstrapped, boots
unlaced, and everyone could sink
knee-deep in a humming splendor.

That's wrong, of course.
History proves it.
Once you reach the final point
of all those roads cut by granite-faced
ancestors and even your own
forgettable efforts, then the spirit
is so stalled by arrival
that the long grasses become a cage,
the long fields blank

linoleum in a gleaming kitchen,
where you wonder how the chairs stand
so empty, and on certain nights,
with your full belly leaned into the sink
and cool water piped over your wrist,
you suddenly long to shove your arm
down the disposal or rest your head

in the trash compactor or just climb
in your not-quite-paid-for wagon
to breathe clouds till you can stop
breathing, stop sitting there and start

worm-farming, that thankless trade
no one wrote back about,
the quiet work for which you were born.

. . . .

Margaret Hasse
(1950–)

A native of South Dakota, Margaret Hasse was educated at Stanford University and the University of Minnesota. The recipient of fellowships from the National Endowment for the Arts, Minnesota State Arts Board, and McKnight Foundation, she has taught in the Minnesota Writers-in-the-Schools Program, the Loft Literary Center, and Minneapolis Community College. Her books include Stars Above, Stars Below *and* In a Sheep's Eye, Darling, *as well as the collaborative play* Sign of a Child.

Bean Fields

They labor along the straight lines of their
parallel rows, the farm boy, the town girl
earning an hourly wage for her college fund,
weeding, staying even with each other,
learning they like each other's smell.

He has the slight acrid burn of green leaves.
She, catnip—residue of shampoo—
her hair streaked shades of brown

like the fizzy tassels at the top of corn.
His Tom body yowls in the backyard

of his brain that he wants that minty weed.
She, too, longs for the end of the row
when they will sit in the bed of the dirty truck
against warm rubber tires, drink
lemonade with tongues so keen

you could map the exact spot where
the sugar of desire does its dream business,
where the lemon pulp—call it
her education plan, his religious training—
persists in its tart denial.

A bean in its ripe casing hangs on a stem,
three fuzzy lumps in its throat. One for the boy,
one for the girl, and one for how the hinge
of what might happen to us swings slightly,
opening here, closing there.

High School Boyfriend

You are home town.
You are all my favorite places
the last summer I grew up.
Every once in a while
I write you in my head
to ask how Viet Nam
and a big name college
came between us.
We tried to stay in touch
through the long distance
hum and fleck of phone calls.

It was inevitable
that I should return
to the small prairie town
and find you
pumping gas, driving truck, measuring lumber,
and we'd exchange weather talk,
never to be able to break through words
and time to say simply:
"Are you as happy
 as I wanted you to be?"

And still I am stirred
by musky cigarette smoke
on a man's brown suede jacket.
Never having admitted the tenderness
of your hands, I feel them now
on all my skin.
Parking on breezy nights,
in cars, floating passageways,
we are tongue and tongue like warm cucumbers.
I would walk backwards
along far country roads
through late evenings, cool as moving water,
heavy as red beer,
to climb into that August.

In the dark lovers' lanes,
you touched my face
and found me there.

.   .   .   .

J. P. WHITE
(1952–)

J. P. White was born in Akron, Ohio, and educated at New College, Colorado State, and Vermont College. Awards for his work include a Bush Foundation Fellowship, the Loft Award of Distinction in Poetry, and three fellowships from the Minnesota State Arts Board. A resident of Deephaven, Minnesota, he has taught at Colorado State University, Eckerd College, and Vermont College, and has published several volumes of poetry, among them In Pursuit of Wings, The Pomegranate Tree Speaks from the Dictator's Garden, *and* The Salt Hour.

Dove

Called a Jumbo Tennessee Flattop in the trade.
But the half-peeled label between her ribs
Reads—Dove, Kalamazoo, Michigan, Gibson guitar.
Found her in a Denver pawnshop, one Sunday.
No strings, no case, hung on the back wall
Between two pegs. Pawnbroker claimed Earl Scruggs,
My king, brought her in with a broken neck.
Varnish swirled, branched with hair-line cracks.
Soundhole ragged from barnstorm flatpicking.
Wood behind the pickguard scooped out, paper thin.
Her wild cherry body smudged, nicked, gouged,
Even plugged twice with mother-of-pearl.
Frets uneven, maybe warped, tuning pegs loose
And worn. Yet she gleamed amidst the heap
As any bird might, and she was cheap.
So, I strung her in my lap, blew tuning notes
Out of a harp I had brought. String by string,
I got her ready, right, and let my hands fly.
Her bass strings burst big as a kettle drum.
Her E fluttered softer than I had ever imagined.
I ran through a G scale, hit my one good run.
Old, young, this bird torn from bluegrass,
Where was she from? She knew I might fail

To play the notes I heard in my head and pitch
Her out. She knew I was only beginning to scale
Out across the far bridges, but that morning
She rose in my hands, light, springing ahead of me
In a flash, my thumb hammering the bass, on, off,
While somewhere below in the high notes
The white bird I love was born again.

Essay on Leaves

I used to love hard physical labor,
cutting and hauling wood, pouring foundations,
digging at a tangled, gummed root
that wouldn't let go under the blows
of a spudbar, even raking the fifty sacks of leaves
from my yard was work I could lean
into with some anticipation,
since it only came once a year and,
even as a suburban man, I could dive into the leaves
to inhale the rot and molds, the old world pathogens
scarred on the undersides, the dusty perfumes
carried in the leafy veins released under my weight.
I loved raking them all together,
the large finger-shaped red oak leaves,
the honey-colored and fire-engine red maples,
the half-dollar-shaped golden cottonwoods,
then watching them spill through my hands
like nuggets dug from scree.
What had fallen in this fallen world
was rising again in the late October winds
and scattering over the lawns
and driveways like bits of brightly colored rags.
After a neck injury I finally
hired out to a young father and his four sons
who pulled up at the curb, unannounced, on a Sunday
    morning,
in a wobbly, rusted truck with spray-painted,

particle-board sides, a homemade suction hose attached
    to a fan,
and a tarp lashed on top.
The sleekly muscled father strapped
a gas-driven power blower to his back,
and once he got it growling,
he never stopped moving. Maybe he'd underbid the job,
or maybe he was falling faster than the leaves
from some unrecoverable sense of things not adding up,
but he roamed from the backyard to the front in a scowl,
berating the boys, urging them on, driving them
through their somnambulant tasks,
yanking a rake out of one boy's hands
to show him how to dig into the leaves with snap,
shouting at another to feed more leaves
into the vacuum that spit them into the tiny, dented truck.
I kept thinking a man who carried such sculpted beauty,
square chin, high cheekbones, broad shoulders,
would turn away from the sparks of his ferocious energy
to administer words of gentle command.
One look into the boys' faces
and you could tell they were nearly broken,
shattered by the long hours, the leaf dirt,
the gasoline roar of the engines,
by their father yelling over all the sound
to make sure his instructions were heard.
They looked unapproachable like runaways
I'd seen in New York on the Tenderloin between 8th and
    Columbus,
all bloodshot milkiness in the eyes,
crouched over a grate, afraid to talk.
These sons lived beyond tears and you could easily imagine
any one of them exploding in an uncontrollable bout
of rage and sorry destruction. In this father's voice,
I heard my own father scaring me when I didn't figure out
some mechanical job as fast as he did, his words
much louder than I could track,

his jagged strength shivering my frame
like a saw skidding through a knot to bite the head of a nail.
I hated his annoyed, sullen bluster while admiring his
    dexterity,
his skill to make things fit together with a wrench
like the diagrams showed.
The fixers of this world were *real men*, I told myself
in a rubbery sway of mesmerized fascination and choked
    anger.
The rest of us broke things, whined about how much repairs
    cost,
when real men figured it out themselves,
no matter how many false starts, busted knuckles.
But where had this father's life gone awry
in the speechless world of real men?
Maybe this father couldn't afford a house
for his children or the payments on his truck.
Maybe his wife was pregnant again and he resented the new
    arrival.
I was not a father, and didn't know the pressure
of all those mouths to feed, doctor bills, the endless shirts,
boots, jackets. I could never enter his pain,
nor could he imagine mine watching him drive his business
on the backs of his children who hunkered near ground
like pack animals buckled on the trail.
I wanted to say to him *maybe you should ease up*
on the crew or you boys like some lemonade and cookies,
something to dispel the heat of meanness that cut
the air like animal catarrh. But I said nothing
when he came to collect, nothing about the boys' bitterness
and dazed sorrow that reminded me
of my own which I used to bury
beneath the many leaves
my father and I had raked together and made ready for fire.

. . . .

DAVID WOJAHN
(1953–)

David Wojahn was born in St. Paul and educated at the University of Min-
nesota and the University of Arizona. His first book, Icehouse Lights,
received the Yale Series of Younger Poets Award and the Poetry Society of
America's William Carlos Williams Award. His second collection, Glass-
works, *was awarded the Society of Midland Authors' Award. Other books*
include Mystery Train, Late Empire, *and* The Falling Hour. *He*
teaches creative writing at Indiana University and in the writing program
at Vermont College.

Fort Snelling National Cemetery:
St. Paul, Minnesota

Thirty thousand dead, the markers all identical,
and with a map I find his stone,
                    find my own name chiseled
here between the monoliths of airport runway lights
and "the world's largest shopping mall," its parking lot

nudging the cemetery fence. The spirit in its tunnel
does not soar, the spirit raised by wolves.

The parable of the cave, the spirit raised
by shades and flickering shadows.
                     Down the grid

of colored lights a Northwest triple seven
lumbers into sleet
            that melts against my father's name

like the striking of a tongueless bell, a code
compact and unabstract as DNA, and with my hand

I trace three times the rough, wet letters.
The jets shriek
        and the rain-slick marble shimmers.

Tribute and Ash

i.
A Landscape by Grant Wood

By an open barn door two cows loll,
A Holstein and a Guernsey, and a white
Horse grazes in the shadows of a hill.

A one-lane bridge, and to its right
A gravel road that winds some feeble
Mashed potato mounds—a Midwest

Effort at terrain, where barns
Outnumber houses, and a bone white church spire
Nudges the left hand frame. Not a *town*,

Not even a hamlet. Grain elevator,
Tavern on the riverbank,
The trio of rickety windmills, water tower,

Willows and some mystery trees that flank
The water, resembling puffballs or grapes.
Each night she'd come home from Northwest Bank,

From her ledgers and adding machine tapes
Littering the floor like barbershop hair.
And under these drab cornfields she'd smoke

The packs of Salem straights, curlers
Shaping their weird corona, romance
Novels and a highball tumbler

Replenished each hour with a splash
Of gin. The endless curlicues
Of smoke. For thirty years she'd cough,

Flip the pages while the white frame grew
The color of a spoiled apple.
A cheap print: not even "sentimental value."

No one bought it at the yard sale.

ii.
Memory Place

Vesalius, scalpel aloft, as he splits like a melon
The hanged man's skull, fragile trepanning to unveil
    some terra
Incognita of the soul, uncover the seat of memory

Which resides in current, in minute sacs of seawater,
Encoded, shot through with electrical charges.
The cerebral cortex halved, dead wings.

No computer, this, to tell me that today
She's been dead three years, an anniversary marked
Unwittingly by purple tulips in a jar, and seven

Days of April rain. Reliquary. Missed connections.
    Sentences
Where no one stares from windows longingly. Sentences
Refusing to describe old photographs. Retrievable

And irretrievable, each fragment in its own
Canopic jar. No need to tell me I reside still in that house
Where she's—say it—by the flowerbed, straw hat flaring

And tied with a yellow scarf. *He died of this too,*
She was saying from the couch, where she had to be propped
In a certain way by the nurse, who'd come each morning

With the morphine. *Who?* I said. *Hubert Humphrey.*
He shook hands with me once at the bank. Always smiling.
This borne to the palaces of memory. Loot and booty,

Tribute and ash. The charnel house of memory. Open me,
Observe. The bone saw's snarl. The edifice
Viewed from above, almost an aerial view. Inject

The sinews with purple dye, to circle and arc the synapses
Like footage of squid. Tentacle, ink screen, the dye vats
Of Tyre. *I never did think much of him, but you could see*

The pain on his face every night on the news. He died
You know at home. Doorways, courtyards, bannisters.
Beyond the room, another room. Beyond the room.

. . . .

DAVID MURA
(1952–)

*A third-generation Japanese American, David Mura was born in St. Paul
and educated at the University of Minnesota and Vermont College. He is the
author of two memoirs, one volume of critical essays, and the poetry collec-
tions* After We Lost Our Way, The Colors of Desire, *and An-
gels for the Burning. He has received two fellowships from the National
Endowment for the Arts, two Bush Foundation Fellowships, several Min-
nesota State Arts Board fellowships, a Lila Wallace–Reader's Digest Writ-
ers Award, the Josephine Miles Book Award, the Carl Sandburg Literary
Award, and a National Poetry Series Prize. A resident of Minneapolis, he
has taught at the University of Minnesota, St. Olaf College, and the Uni-
versity of Oregon.*

Harvest at Minidoka Internment Camp

after a watercolor by Kenjiro Nomura, circa 1943

Fingering the crescent pea pods, their squeaky skin,
bending and rising, ripped from the vines, fingering,
becoming, in a line, a line of motion, all one and green,

and slicing through the far mountains, a cumulus stream,
sunlight washes over you, over us, *okaa-san, nee-san*.
And giggling children draw rings in dust by the barracks,

watch the women, mornings, when the peas are pearled
with dew, glistening as foreheads glisten towards noon,
kerchiefs binding brows, the harvest flicked to baskets,

their implements burnished with callus, hard and delicate
as diamonds, sharp as steel, fingers that wash an infant's
    smile.
Everything flows, fox gloves at field's edge, river beyond
    wires,

a line of bodies, like shadows of clouds, shifting down rows,
and the chorus they sang—" . . . under the apple tree,"
    "*sakura*"—
how can I know? (And all the while, I know mother knows.)

Minidoka, I recall only this woman I knew for years. Peas
she set steaming, tumbling before me, tiny indented pebbles
I pushed about. How I refused. Her voice measured, cold.

The Angel of Phillips Park

Two crows in the alley garbage, shrieking
and scuffling at a leg bone or stale egg sandwich,
and the night, impatient, takes them down,
their raucous throats and wing flurry now silent.

Night of the first lilacs. Just after a strong spring rain.
Wiping out for a few hours the dealers at the corner,
fists in their baggy pants, Nikes sliding the walk,
black hoods or knit caps, bleary eyes catching it all.

In the park on Franklin, outside the Four Winds School,
the last kid, on the scholarship of his mind, pops

the air with arcs, trey after trey, counting the final
seconds of his game, and the crowd roars in his ears

like the ocean he's never seen, and just as he hits
the top of the key, the first shot steels through
the sternum, one then his shooting hand, so quick
pulling the trigger, and it flows from the porous spot

draining his belly like a black hole in the heavens,
and on this court where he always won and gave it all,
his body topples in a puddle so epic and slow in its fall,
some bit of his brain's still hot, *Made it, nothing but net.*

Silence now, stepping through wet grass. Held in check
till the flashing lights and the tires of the city's finest
screech to the tennis courts. The static on the radio
mikes 10–4 breaking up. The crows start at it again.

And no one sees one rising higher and higher on wings
of blackness and prayer, a jam so devastating
and powerful, redeeming all the light in this universe
and giving it back as a crow, a night, a boy, a star.

Minneapolis Public

There are 150 first languages in our schools
and so many aliens even E.T. would go unnoticed,
though if your tongue moved one way in the land of your
      birth
it must move another now, awkward at first.

There are blacks here who've never been to Africa;
Africans who've never heard a Baptist prayer,
much less the solemn dirges of Lutherans
or how the artist formerly known is some sort of Prince.

In the anthology of American Buddhist poetry
you will find not one face of a Tibetan
but they are here with girls and boys named Tenzin
and one, my son's good friend, throws a hard mean spiral.

Esmir is not the name of a girl but a Bosnian
boy who crouches at a table and glues a lamp together
and later with my other son conspires on a book—"A Touch
of Rabies"—a heartbreaking tale of good dogs gone bad.

(Why tell a soul of the sieges that brought him here
or stories of the Dali Lama and the temples destroyed
or troops of the warlords in the streets of Somalia,
the borders dividing death from safety if not evil and good?)

Say you're Egyptian or Haitian: Here you're singular,
not part of a Big Apple ghetto. If you're Chinese,
most likely you're adopted, or else your parents study
engineering at the U. And have I mentioned the Mexicans?
In *West Side Story* the rumble starts with Puerto Ricans
and working-class whites in a high-school gym;
this year Maria's still Natalie Wood white to Jamaica's
half-black Anita, and the jets sport blacks, one Tibetan,

and my *happa* daughter who still doesn't question
such casting, or why *Bye Bye Birdie* last year
just might not be the choice of half the school
for a song and dance they could take on as their own.

Still at the spring school dance J.Lo and Ja Rule
set the awkward bump and grind of junior high girls
and the boys watch on the sidelines as boys that age do,
whether Bosnian, black, white, Somali, Tibetan.

I'm told we live in the Land of Great Lake Wobegon
where all the women are strong, the men good-looking,
and the children above average—and, I always add,

everyone's white. Hey, Tenzin, Nabil, go tell Garrison:
Not now. Not quite.

.   .   .   .

Louise Erdrich
(1955–)

*A member of the Turtle Mountain Band of Ojibwe, Louise Erdrich was
raised in Wahpeton, North Dakota, and attended Dartmouth College. She
is the author of ten novels, several children's books, and a memoir of early
motherhood. Her poetry collections include* Jacklight, Baptism of De-
sire, *and* Original Fire: Selected and New Poems. *She has received
the Nelson Algren Award and the National Book Critics Circle Award for
her novel* Love Medicine. *She lives in Minneapolis and is co-owner, with
her sister Heid E. Erdrich, of Birchbark Books Press.*

Dear John Wayne

August and the drive-in picture is packed.
We lounge on the hood of the Pontiac
surrounded by the slow-burning spirals they sell
at the window, to vanquish the hordes of mosquitoes.
Nothing works. They break through the smoke screen for
    blood.

Always the lookout spots the Indians first,
spread north to south, barring progress.
The Sioux or some other Plains bunch
in spectacular columns, ICBM missiles,
feathers bristling in the meaningful sunset.

The drum breaks. There will be no parlance.
Only the arrows whining, a death-cloud of nerves
swarming down on the settlers

who die beautifully, tumbling like dust weeds
into the history that brought us all here
together: this wide screen beneath the sign of the bear.

The sky fills, acres of blue squint and eye
that the crowd cheers. His face moves over us,
a thick cloud of vengeance, pitted
like the land that was once flesh. Each rut,
each scar makes a promise: *It is*
not over, this fight, not as long as you resist.

Everything we see belongs to us.

A few laughing Indians fall over the hood
slipping in the hot spilled butter.
The eye sees a lot, John, but the heart is so blind.
Death makes us owners of nothing.
He smiles, a horizon of teeth
the credits reel over, and then the white fields

again blowing in the true-to-life dark.
The dark films over everything.
We get into the car
scratching our mosquito bites, speechless and small
as people are when the movie is done.
We are back in our skins.

How can we help but keep hearing his voice,
the flip side of the sound track, still playing:
Come on, boys, we got them
where we want them, drunk, running.
They'll give us what we want, what we need.
Even his disease was the idea of taking everything.
Those cells, burning, doubling, splitting out of their skins.

The Buffalo Prayer

Our Lady of the Buffalo Bones, pray for us.
Our Lady of the bales of skins and rotting hulks
from which our tongues alone were taken,
pray for us, Our Lady of the Poisoned Meat
and of the wolves who ate
and whose tongues swelled until they burst.
Our Lady of the Eagles Dropping from the Sky,
Our Lady of the Sick Fox and of the Lurching Hawk
and of the hunters at the edge of Yellowstone Park waiting
to rain thunder on the last of us.
Pray for us, Our Lady of Polaris.
Our Lady of the Sleek Skidoo.
Our Lady of Destruction Everywhere
Our bones were ground into fertilizer
for the worn-out eastern earth.
Our bones were burned to charcoal
to process sugar and to make glue
for the shoe soles of your nuns and priests.
Our Lady of the Testicle Tobacco Pouch
Our Lady of the Box Cars of Skulls,
pray for us whose bones have nourished
the ordered cornfields that have replaced
the random grass
which fed and nurtured and gave us life.

Rez Litany

Let us now pray to those beatified
within the Holy Colonial church
beginning with Saint Assimilus,
patron of residential and of government
boarding schools, whose skin was dark
but who miraculously bled white milk
for all to drink.

To cure the gut aches that resulted
as ninety percent of Native children are
lactose intolerant, let us now pray to the
patron saint of the Indian Health Service,
who is also guardian of slot machines,
Our Lady of Luck, she who carries
in one hand mistaken blood tests and botched
surgeries and in the other hand the heart
of a courageous doctor squeezed dry.
Let us pray for the sacred hearts of all good doctors
and nurses, whose tasks are manifold and made more
    difficult
by the twin saints of commodity food,
Saint Bloatinus and Saint Cholestrus,
who were martyred at the stake of body fat
and who preside now in heaven
at the gates of the Grand Casino Buffet.
Saint Macaronia and Saint Diabeta, hear our prayer.
It is terrible to be diminished toe by toe.
Good Saint Pyromane,
Enemy of the BIA,
Deliver us from those who seek to bury us
in files and triplicate documents and directives.
Saint Quantum, Martyr of Blood
and Holy Protector of the Tribal Rolls,
assist us in the final shredding which shall proceed
on the Day of Judgment so we may all rain down
in a blizzard of bum pull tabs
and unchosen lottery tickets, which represent
the souls of the faithfully departed
in your name.
Your name written in the original fire
we mistook so long ago for trader's rum.
Pray for us, all you saints of white port
four roses old granddad and night train.
Good Saint Bingeous who fell asleep upside down on the
    cross

and rose on the third day without even knowing he had
    died:
Saint Odium of the hundred-proof blood
and Saint Tremens of the great pagan spiders
dripping from the light fixtures.
You powerful triumvirate, intercede for us
drunks stalled in the bars,
float our asses off the cracked stools
and over to the tribal college,
where the true saints are ready to sacrifice their brain cells
for our brain cells, in that holy exchange which is called
    learning.
Saint Microcephalia, patron of huffers and dusters,
you of the cooked brain and mean capacity, you
of the simian palm line and poor impulse control,
you of the Lysol-soaked bread, you sleeping with the dogs
underneath the house, hear our prayers
which we utter backwards and sideways
as nothing makes sense
least of all your Abstinence Campaign
from which Oh Lord Deliver Us.
Saints Primapara, Gravida, and Humpenenabackseat,
you patrons of unsafe teenage sex
and fourteen-year-old mothers,
pray for us now and at the hour of our birth,
amen.

1985–Present

•   •   •   •   •

SHARON CHMIELARZ
(1940–)

A native of Mobridge, South Dakota, Sharon Chmielarz graduated from the University of Minnesota with degrees in education, German, and English. A recipient of fellowships from the Minnesota State Arts Board and the Jerome Foundation, she is the author of the poetry collections Different Arrangements, But I Won't Go Out in a Boat, Stranger in Her House, The Other Mozart, *and* The Rhubarb King, *as well as of the children's books* Down at Angel's, End of Winter, *and* Pied Piper of Hamelin. *She is a longtime resident of Minneapolis.*

Like a Church

Like a church on the North Sea,
the Berlin Baptist
stands on a hilltop,
a spare, big-boned house looking
over a sea of marsh and fields.

The walls run a good
fist thick
against the tides
of wind.
Two bars,
gun-barrel thin,
prop up the window frame.

Mullions square off the glass.
In the theology of rods they come
from four directions at once
to tame, bind and confound
the scope of the vision
as well as to divide
the immensity of the Great
Plains into parcels—

each pane, a handspan
wide. What light
falls in, remains,
the messenger from heaven,
underfoot among fixed benches.

On Sundays my grandfather comes to sing.
Pumped music rolls just over the tops of high notes.
His voice rolls like a breaker just under the crest,
all the way down to the end of a song and will not be rushed.

In the pause between hymns
you can hear the wind,
the sound of the farm,
the people I come from.
And its taste on the tongue is grit.

They Come Humming

What is the keyboard
but a variation on a table,
a trough in ivory and ebony
for all the Hungry
to come and be
soothed by food's music—

    his head is bowed.
    Like the pianist at an old Knabe,
    Grandfather Gottlieb at the table
    flexes his thick, speckled fingers
    over the plate and begins to hum
    for the 15,633rd time,
    "Komm, Herr Jesu, sei unser Gast
    und segne was Du uns bescheret hast.
    Amen." Then he lifts

fork and knife to the sausage and
snaps the fried skin.

Eating is a reminder of
your link in the Great Chain of Being,
though Grandfather, *der Gottlieb*,
never knew life by that name.

I do and I sit alone.
Remembering the power
in rings and chains
I set no place at my table
for old names, but still
they come, down aisles
in waist-high wheatfields
towards my table, singlefile,
out of groves of ashes,
black-scarfed serfs
with a ring in one ear,
big-bellied, German-Russians,
they come humming.

.   .   .   .

JIM HEYNEN
(1940–)

Jim Heynen was born on a farm near Sioux Center, Iowa, and educated at Calvin College and the universities of Oregon and Iowa. The recipient of numerous awards, including a National Endowment for the Arts Fellowship and the U.S.–U.K. Bicentennial Fellowship, he has taught at many universities throughout the country, including the University of Alaska, the University of Oregon, and Metropolitan State University in St. Paul. His books include The Man Who Kept Cigars in His Cap, A Suitable Church,

You Know What Is Right, The One-Room Schoolhouse, *and* The Boy's House.

The Forest

When the grandfather returned from his trip out West to see relatives, he had big news for the boys. He took them on their usual walk down the path between the cornfields and the pasture. He reached for a corn tassel, rolled the pollen in his hands, and sprinkled it across other cornstalks as they walked. Then he said, Would you believe there are probably more trees in the world than stalks of corn?

The boys looked at the half-mile-long rows of corn, all the tassels swaying in the sun. Hundreds and thousands of corn tassels as far as their eyes could see.

Their grandfather told of travelling through mountains where all he could see were miles of slopes longer than corn rows covered with trees. Trees, trees, trees, he said.

Where did they plant the corn with all those trees? asked one boy.

There was no corn in the forests, he said. Just trees, trees, and more trees.

Didn't that get boring? asked the boy.

Their grandfather reached for another corn tassel, held this one to his nose, then rubbed it between his palms more slowly than before. Yes, he said. That's why I came back early.

Butterflies

When the men were out working in the fields, it was easy to tell them apart. Even if you couldn't see their faces or if you weren't close enough to make out their size and shape, the way they moved was enough to show who they were. If one bent over to pull a thistle or leaned his elbow on a fence post, it was as if he were writing his name on the air in big letters—it was so clear who he was.

But on Sundays, when the men were dressed in dark suits and sitting on the church pews, they looked alike. All those suntanned faces up to the white forehead where the hat band started. And during congregational prayer when they bowed their heads together, they seemed to turn into plants that had budded in a field of straight rows. The only way you could tell who was who was by remembering where each one always sat.

But when the worshipping was over and they walked out of the rose-windowed church, they were like butterflies coming out of cocoons. All their different colors got brighter and clearer as they went back into the sun toward the sparkling fields. One by one in their own ways they became themselves again.

Sheds

Down the road lived a man who was an odd one. He built seventy sheds on his farm. Little sheds, where he could put little things everyone figured could go somewhere else. Whenever he had something he wanted to put away, instead of looking for a place for it in one of his buildings, he built a special little shed to put it in. When he bought a new lawn mower, he built a new shed for it. When his dog had eight puppies, he built eight little doghouses for the new animals. He had a little shed where he put tin cans. He had one for old shoes. This man had built a separate shed for chicken feathers.

But one shed, way back in the grove, painted bright red with white trim, was his secret shed.

What does he keep in that red shed in the grove? everyone wondered.

The boys sneaked out there to find out, but the red shed had a big lock on it. And no windows to see through.

So they went to the man and asked him, What do you have in your red shed in the grove? He was a friendly enough man, so they thought it would be all right to ask.

But the man got angry when the boys asked him this and said, That is none of your business, none at all.

When the boys went back to check the shed again, the man had put another lock on the door and a sign that said KEEP OUT.

Let's climb up in one of those trees and wait, said one of the boys. Maybe he'll come by and unlock the door.

They climbed the tree and sat on branches where they could see the man's shed.

Pretty soon he came out there. He was carrying two keys. He knelt down in front of his shed and un-locked one lock. Then the other. He opened the door of his secret shed.

Inside was another shed! A blue one that had a lock on its door, too. Then he opened the door of the blue shed, and inside was a smaller yellow shed! And inside that a green one! The man was down on his knees opening door after door of his little sheds. Pretty soon the boys couldn't see where his hand was going. And all those little sheds, one after another, looked like a rainbow, and the boys couldn't see where it ended.

· · · ·

DIANE GLANCY
(1941–)

Diane Glancy was born in Kansas City, Missouri, to a mother of English and German descent and a father of Cherokee descent. The recipient of numerous awards for her work, including a McKnight Artist Fellowship, a Loft-McKnight Award of Distinction in Creative Prose, a Lannan Foundation Fellowship, a Minnesota Book Award, and an American Book Award, she is the author of the novels Designs of the Night Sky *and* The Man Who Heard the Land, *of the essay collections* The Cold-and-Hunger Dance *and* Claiming Breath, *and of the poetry volumes* The Relief of America, Iron Woman, *and* Offering. *From 1987 until her retirement in 2004, she taught Native American literature and creative writing at Macalester College.*

How

Sleeping Face & Old Bull Thigh,
a row of beaver bones for a rib-
vest, a canoe-shaped smile, sit
in the shade & say the ancestors
came to the new world bobbing
under sealskin floats on the land-
bridge under the Bering Straits.
They hunted mammoths, planted
maize & beans & squash & the sky
seemed clear was soon crammed
with clouds, every corner of it,
like settlers' wagons & then
farmers' sheds built with scraps
& stuffed with cultivators & hay
& the dust storm with lightning
sparklers rolled up the prairie
with its night & how swatting flies
the ancestors must have wondered
what land bridge the white man

crossed, what mammoth he followed
from the other way.

Pow Wow

She wore a buckskin sewn with elk teeth ➤ beaded
moccasins & leggings with turtle shell rattles at
her ankles ➤ she had a beaver skin bag ➤ shawl
she wore ➤ silver bracelets ➤ beads ➤ a belt
with a squirrel-head buckle ➤ the holes in her
ears studded with ornaments ➤ hair braided ➤
cheeks painted red & the part in her hair ➤
beaded headband ➤ feathers in her braids ➤ she
rode in the coupe a box of maple sugars in her lap ➤
deerhorns on the hood ➤ striped blankets
over the seats ➤ she did the little dance of
women the mince-step inside the circle of men
ranting with their dance but she ➤ painted woman
took one step then another not much more than a
hen pecking for grain ➤ the feet slightly moving
to the drum ➤ eyes on the ground ➤ fringed shawl
folded over her arm ➤ the beaded bag & feather-
fan on her wrist ➤ & what of the woman who could
birth a child beside the trail get up & migrate
with the tribe ➤ who heard the pines moan ➤ saw
the wood barns for animals ➤ the settlers sod
farmers ➤ their basins buckets rattling in their
wagons & old trucks ➤ the clangs they made with
tin & metal ➤ their ladle feet ➤ the river brush
of their beards ➤ her thoughts returned to the ➤
circle dance ➤ the tiny bells on her sash ➤ the
turtle shell rattles the sound of drums in her
head ➤ the men around her powwowed ➤ the Great
Spirit poked her ➤ the sky flew with her prayers
➤ swallows splittails ➤ all splendor ➤ Lord of
fleas & spiders ➤ bless the tongues that dance

with song ➤ the claws of bear muskrats otter
weasel skunk tortoise ➤ bless the beans squash
the nuts acorns wild roots ➤ the tree bark ➤
horses' ears ➤ old bones full of worms they ➤
boiled & pounded to mortar ➤ ate in the night of
their hunger.

. . . .

PHILIP BRYANT
(1951–)

Philip Bryant was born and raised in Chicago, Illinois, and educated at Gustavus Adolphus College in St. Peter and Columbia University. He has taught at Chicago State University and Harold Washington College, and is presently on the faculty of English at Gustavus Adolphus. A recipient of a Minnesota State Arts Board Fellowship, he is the author of Blue Island, Sermon on a Perfect Spring Day, *and* South Side Suite, *a suite of poetry and jazz with composer and pianist Carolyn Wilkins.*

Stella by Starlight

My mother couldn't understand how my father, a man
stuffed so full of promise and potential, could wither
it all away on a stack of bebop records and a bottle of
beer. And his close friend, Preston, was worse—un-
dereducated and couldn't speak the King's English if
you'd held a gun to his head, gave him the book, and
asked him to quote any passage out of Shakespeare.
Every other word was *muthafuck* this or *muthafuck* that.
Why my father associated with him, who in my
mother's opinion was far beneath him, was an open
mystery, something beyond her. Jazz, Jazz, Jazz, that's
all she heard—*morning, noon,* and *night*—when he could

have easily risen to be a great surgeon, lawyer, or civil rights leader. But one day I walked in on them by accident and there they were: Preston and my dad, a little drunk, crouched over the turntable. I understood why when they turned around, taken completely by surprise for an instant. I saw that both their dark faces reflected the light and were shining.

Poincianna

Somewhere on a hot
and stormy Saturday night
in Kasota, Minnesota,
"Poincianna" is playing
on the radio
above the kitchen stove.
The electric mixer
is left on and forgotten
as it whips cake batter
all over the walls and floor—
a balding, middle-aged man
in just his T-shirt and boxer shorts
and his plump, aproned-wife
slowdance in the dim summer light,
as the yellow and white daisies
outside in the garden
feverishly shutter
and shake at the sound
of falling rain.

Gray Strands of Hair

to Renée

It's a
poor excuse

for a
violin string.
If you
stretch it
that far,
it would break
in two
without even
a popping
sound.
When you comb it out
and then, later
in bed,
when I touch
a gray strand
in the dark,
it suddenly crackles.
"Electricity,"
you say
nonchalantly,
as it throws off
little sparks
between us—
still,
after some
twenty-odd
years together.

. . . .

RICHARD ROBBINS
(1953–)

*A native of Los Angeles, California, Richard Robbins was educated at San
Diego State University and the University of Montana. Awards for his work
include a National Endowment for the Arts Fellowship, a Minnesota State*

Arts Board Fellowship, the Kay Sexton Award, and the Loft-McKnight Poetry of Distinction Award. Director of the Creative Writing Program at Minnesota State University at Mankato, he is the author of The Invisible Wedding *and* Famous Persons We Have Known.

He Confuses the Grandchild for the Son

And who would blame him,
at 85, for what's a slip of the tongue
anyway, memory—especially for names—
no longer automatic, the joy
of talk alive in his mouth, running ahead of all

other faculties. Oh, he may piece
two lifetimes into one,
but sickness takes a different course, the world so singular
it's lonely. I've seen men his age
make of themselves the cold stones of fields

distanced from the rest
by life mimicking the imagined life
of death. Their children
fear silence because of them. They dip their hands
into rivers bitter with acid—
only the bones remain.

Now when he calls me Bob,
reminds me
of a 30-pound trout I never caught,
I tell him my uncle
landed that one, that my son is walking.
When he stops for a moment, I say
Keenan, and the words all
become arranged again, there with those
that never lag: *Marie, Pocatello,*

caul, corm, bougainvillaea, Canada wind,
Mojave, kokanee. Around them
the circle keeps

drawing itself for the dizzied still loving.

After the Miracle

A gate in the spine open, muscles there
gone slack as clothesline, finally and now
strangely her back doesn't exist, the pain
swept away as cleanly as the factory's

acid air once the wind shifts. She sits,
remembering tightness, the way it drew
all of her to its center, distracting
any motion, any other thought. After

the miracle, after the all of her
focused inward suddenly disappeared,
what was there left but doubt in the new walk
and restored axis? Fearing ease, braced

for the wrong step that would freeze her to her
spasm—come home again, familiar—
what were the yard and house but background again
to inward attention, this time on absence,

on the emptiness of her without pain,
while the dumb flesh spread out, and body hair
twisted toward light, and grass filled the yard,
and lawn, trees, and gate opened to the street?

Near Roslin Institute, Midlothian, Scotland

birthplace of the cloned sheep Dolly

Under the groined roofs of Rosslyn Chapel,
a man plays bagpipes in stone while Abraham
sharpens his knife. Across the lintel falls
King Darius, asleep, dragon attacks
imminent at every pillar despite
the best wishes of carved cleric or king,
despite corporal works of mercy, prayers
the ploughman might send up, or husband, wife,
carpenter, gardener, sportsman, child on knees
next to its own skeleton, the farmer—

each too wrapped by Vice or The Dance of Death
to be saved. Blessed are they, then, for stories
telling themselves upward from stone. Past the mouths
of snakes, a dog leads the blind man to glory.
Doves with olive leaves sweep over his head.
A seated lady prays for him. A warrior
battles, a monk drinks for the coming crown.
Christ is dying everywhere for the dead.
And near each stained glass an angel hovers
in its light with scroll, cross, or book—open

at one niche, closed at the next—the story
turning inward, outward, all in color
blazing through saints. No wonder, too, history
must reject this place. Its business to suffer
more than believe, to act larger than hope,
and smaller, it makes the counter-legends
to the Grail locked in these foundations. It
needs to repeat itself, first to last cup
and back, while two fields away, quite decent
men walk a lamb into light without origin.

. . . .

JOYCE SUTPHEN
(1949–)

Joyce Sutphen was born and raised on a farm near St. Joseph and was edu-cated at the University of Minnesota. Currently teaching at Gustavus Adolphus College in St. Peter, she has received many awards for her work, including the Barnard New Women Poets Prize, the Tietjens Award from Poetry Magazine, *a Loft-McKnight Award, a Minnesota State Arts Board Fellowship, and a Minnesota Book Award. Her books include* Straight Out of View, Coming Back to the Body, *and* Naming the Stars.

Home to the Late Late Movie

This landscape like a supermarket aisle
draws me on. Flat and stocked
rows of suburbia, matchbox cars parked
in the driveways, frail little trees
strung tight and anchored to the yards.

And the snowmobiles rusting beside the garage,
and the chainlink fence with the shadow
lunging back and forth all morning, and the
plastic big-wheels on the graveled edge
of the road, white-blond hair of blue-eyed

Boys flirting with speed, pedaling their way
into traffic, looking over their shoulders
to the houses set uncertainly in the cornfields,
their mothers held captive by afternoon TV,
loneliness seeping through the vinyl blinds.

Until the fathers come home from the car shop,
from the lumber yard, from the freezer factory,
garage doors lifting, chains jerking in tracks,
the blond boys running across fat patches of grass,
the daughters glancing up from their books.

And sighs like ovens and the clatter of dinner
plates coming from kitchens, a sizzling in the pan,
stainless steel lifted to the mouth, the smoke of
conversations drifting from the chimneys, dissipating
over the gray branches of the leafless wind.

And later on these streets: in each house with
its drapes parted slightly, wafer of lamplight
caught on bare walls, blue of a video eye
flickering its gaze back into the night, the
refrigerators are opening, letting out the cold.

Death Becomes Me

Death has been checking me out,
making himself at home in my body,
as if he needed to know his way
through the skin, faintly rippling
over the cheekbone to the hollow
beneath my eyes, loosening
the tightly wound ligaments
in the arm, the leg,
infirming the muscle
with his subtle caress,
traveling along the nerve,
leaping from one synapse
to the next, weaving his dark threads
into the chord that holds me tall.
Death is counting my hair,
figuring out the linear equation
of my veins and arteries,
the raised power
of a million capillaries,
acquainting himself with the
calculus of my heart,
accessing the archives

of memory, reading them
forward and backward,
finding his name everywhere.
Death comes to rest in my womb,
slaking away the rich velvet
of those walls, silently halting
the descending pearls,
as if he could burrow in
and make himself my mother,
as if he could bare my bones
and bring me to that other birth.

Getting the Machine

It was good to hear
my own voice again
when I called, after
being gone for weeks.
I sounded about the same.
I hadn't changed my name;
didn't have a foreign accent.
I just said I couldn't
come to the phone right then,
exactly the way I'd been
saying it for years,
and so I left myself
a little message
saying how sorry
I was I wasn't there,
and that I'd be
home soon. I tried to
think of what I'd want
to hear myself saying
and say it right.

.   .   .   .

DALE JACOBSON
(1950–)

A native of Fergus Falls, Minnesota, Dale Jacobson was educated at Minnesota State University at Moorhead and the University of North Dakota. He is the author of Dakota Incantations, Poems for Goya's Disparates, Hunting My Home Town, Factories and Cities, *and* A Walk by the River, *among others. A resident of Moorhead, he has taught at Fort Yates Community College, Hamline University, Moorhead, and the University of North Dakota, where he currently teaches in the department of English.*

from *A Walk by the River*

in dark essential correspondence
Jorge Carrera Andrade

However they came, by whatever long
and strange passage through the dark
biologies, the voices sing—
trill,
     hum,
          warble, serenade, hiss,
cry out,
       voices . . .
            a traffic of callings,
through the traveling day, along the roads,
the haunting coo of the mourning dove,
born from the dark of a hollow log,
the jay whose shrill cry like a glass knife
shatters serenity,
         the crazy crow caw
an alarm seeking a riot, notes in the dusk:
night hawk,
      meadow lark,
           insect distances...
and in the houses with their liquid windows

where the moonlight swims,
                      voices
behind the doors, speaking to be known
as though being heard—saved.
Voices clear as the cricket cry
inside the vault of evening, they are
calls from beneath the ocean's
collapsing wave—each word
a revolt, hammer or drum building a stair
or another dimension—voices
raised or whispered against the pale hour
of old wood becoming the weather,
nails escaping through rusty holes,
the futility of abandoned buildings
with disorder loosening their seams,
voices that refuse the defeat
of fatal places where silence
enfolds solitude
                and ghosts of birds
close their wings to become stones
on the dark side of the moon.

And I know of voices lost—
                 people
lost . . .
      voices that never spoke,
cut down by death squads,
censored by the habit of fear,
voices traveling down alleys,
mumbling to themselves—
                or rolling off
the roofs of bedrooms like dreams of rain,
or flying through the nightmare cities
where clocks put on grotesque faces,
secretive voices falling within themselves,
keeping company with autumn leaves
that swirl around a hollow center
like a ghost hunting its shape,

voices anonymous as a field of wheat,
or chaff, mute labor, worn-out tools,
voices awaiting the hour of speech:

in the lost cities the lost citizens,
their silences shredded by sirens,
a world calling to itself—
                              tearing itself apart—
poverties, despairs, the inheritances of anger
that cannot surrender—slums where people
live and lose in the laid-low wreckages
landlords call 'rental properties,'
a world demolishing itself from neglect—
voices await the invention of a word—

or:
      from the sharp-shattered ruin of all work
when the slow war becomes sudden,
when power stumbles over its broken mask,
and killing is a way of life, then
in the intervals when the bombings cease,
the subtleties of shadow and quiet
conspire a world that can *hear* a word—
(a world calling to itself)—
remote origins, calling:
the ancient energies:
                              we are: the need to speak
across the empty spaces between us,
and say:
the houses of the stars are open, the day is wide.

In the far distance I hear children calling
from their world of play. Who can say
where one voice ends, another begins?

.   .   .   .

DAVID MASON
(1954–)

David Mason grew up in Bellingham, Washington, and received his education at Colorado College and the University of Rochester in New York. From 1989 to 1998, he taught in the department of English at Minnesota State University at Moorhead. In 1994, he was named Minnesota Professor of the Year by the Carnegie Endowment for the Advancement of Higher Education, and also won a Minnesota State Arts Board Grant. He is the author and editor of numerous books, including The Buried Houses *(winner of the Nicholas Roerich Poetry Prize),* The Country I Remember *(winner of the Alice Fay DiCastagnola Award),* Arrivals, *and* The Poetry of Life and the Life of Poetry: Essays and Reviews. *He teaches at Colorado College in Colorado Springs.*

The Pond

Downcast thermometers record one truth
of winter, though the clear light hints of spring.
The furnace blows a warming reverie
where I drop anchor somewhere in the woods
with a girl I haven't seen for twenty years.

I find the pond secluded in the park,
filled by a waterfall beside a bluff
where we held hands and jumped, yelling love,
laughing to find ourselves alive again
and young as always, touching each other's skin.

Tonight the temperature is due to fall,
an arctic stillness settle on the prairies . . .
The years slow down and look about for shelter
far from forests and far from summer ponds:
the mind ghosting out in a shoal of stars.

The Lost House

A neighbor girl went with me near the creek,
entered the new house they were building there
with studs half-covered. Alone in summer dark,
we sat together on the plywood floor.

The shy way I contrived it, my right hand
slipped insinuatingly beneath her blouse
in new maneuvers, further than I planned.
I thought we floated in that almost-house.

Afraid of what might happen, or just afraid,
I stopped. She stood and brushed the sawdust off.
Fifteen that summer, we knew we could have strayed.
Now, if I saw it in a photograph,

I couldn't tell you where that new house stood.
One night the timbered hillside thundered down
like a dozen freight trains, crashing in a flood
that splintered walls and made the owners run.

By then I had been married and divorced.
The girl I reached for in unfinished walls
had moved away as if by nature's course.
The house was gone. Under quiet hills

the creek had cut new banks, left silt in bars
that sprouted alder scrub. No one would know,
cruising the dead-end road beneath the stars,
how we had trespassed there so long ago.

.   .   .   .

JAMES ARMSTRONG
(1957–)

*Born and raised in Indiana and Michigan, James Armstrong holds degrees
from Northwestern, Western Michigan, and Boston universities. He has
taught English and creative writing at Northwestern University and in the
Master of Fine Arts program at the School of the Art Institute of Chicago.
He is the author of* Monument in a Summer Hat, Purl, *and* Blue
Lash. *Awards for his work include the PEN-New England Discovery Prize
for poetry, an Illinois Arts Council Fellowship, and a Minnesota State Arts
Board Fellowship. Since 1999, he has served as professor of English at
Winona State University in Winona.*

The Wreck

for Dot

In the calm of Murray Bay, the island inverts itself:
the brush-tips of pines reach into a wavering sky
through which the sand bottom gleams, as in double
    exposure.
Three times a day the tour boat crosses the harbor

to pause at the wreck-buoys over the *Bermuda*—
I can hear the megaphone, faintly, over the water.
Through the glass bottom, tourists look with interest
at drowned deck timbers, the green yawn of the hatchway.

Lake Superior: Graveyard of the Lakes
says the map we bought, labeled "historically correct."
On the lake's lupine silhouette, the little drawings of
    downed ships
cruise the black water: a flotilla of ghosts.

Sloop or ketch, whaleback, surf tug, lake freighter—
coffins in the damp, now; names to remember:

the *Colorado,* the *Sunbeam,* the *Samuel Foster,*
the *Harry Steinbrenner,* the *George M. Cox,* the *Prussia,*

the *South Shore,* the *Starruca, Kiowa,* and *Servia,*
the *Batchawanna,* the *Golspie* and the *Grace*—
testaments to the romance of disaster
and the exactitude of marine insurance.

You read them nonstop,
in paperbacks bought at the gift shop,
those tales, whose narratives always begin
in sunlight, in mild weather, the captain optimistic—

despite the heavy foreshadowing.
They work their way to the predictable end:
lifeboats overturned, the water boiling with objects,
propellers spinning incongruously in the air

as the ship begins her *long sleigh ride to the bottom.*
In every tale, the lake is the superb antagonist,
covetous, secretive, predatory.
Her numb embrace drags the unwary down:

a truer plot than our official optimism.
What the sea teaches, any sailor knows:
the world's appetite for us is unslakeable.
Our mistake is in thinking we can't drown.

But I can't explain why you've come to love it,
our nightly reading: *the ship was torn in half*
and sank in just eight minutes, with all hands.
Or: *Horrified we watched her burn to the waterline.*

Not for you, the rabbit salads of Beatrix Potter.
People were crying out among the wreckage,
and then there was only silence—
by the time the Coast Guard reached them, it was too late.

When we got back downstate,
you wanted a shipwreck party for your birthday.
Your friends sat on the carpet wearing life jackets
while I read stories about haunted lighthouses

and Flying Dutchmen. A video of the *Titanic*
hushed them: a series of still photographs
taken by sailors of the recovered dead,
their ashen, indrawn faces.

And then the cake: the hull of the HMS *Brittanic*
sculpted in buttercream, tinted a lurid blue
as though submerged fathoms down in the Adriatic.
You blew all eight candles out,

just beginning to know that without warning
the raked bow of the world looms out of the fog—
already the horizon urges you toward the voyage
we all take, from which none of us return.

. . . .

CONNIE WANEK
(1952–)

*Born in Madison, Wisconsin, Connie Wanek grew up on a farm outside
Green Bay until the early 1960s, when her family moved to Las Cruces, New
Mexico. Since 1990, she has lived in Duluth, where she works in the Duluth
Public Library and assists her husband in his work renovating old houses.
The author of* Bonfire *and* Hartley Field, *she has received fellowships
from the Jerome Foundation, the Arrowhead Regional Arts Council, and
the Witter Bynner Foundation.*

After Us

I don't know if we're in the beginning or in the final stage.
Tomas Tranströmer

Rain is falling through the roof.
And all that prospered under the sun,
the books that opened in the morning
and closed at night, and all day
turned their pages to the light;

the sketches of boats and strong forearms
and clever faces, and of fields
and barns, and of a bowl of eggs,
and lying across the piano
the silver stick of a flute; everything

invented and imagined,
everything whispered and sung,
all silenced by cold rain.

The sky is the color of gravestones.
The rain tastes like salt, and rises
in the streets like a ruinous tide.
We spoke of millions, of billions of years.
We talked and talked.

Then a drop of rain fell
into the sound hole of the guitar, another
onto the unmade bed. And after us,
the rain will cease or it will go on falling,
even upon itself.

Hartley Field

And place is always and only place
And what is actual is actual only for one time
And only for one place . . .
T. S. Eliot

The wind cooled as it crossed the open pond
and drove little waves toward us,
brisk, purposeful waves
that vanished at our feet—such energy
thwarted by so little elevation.
The wind was endless, seamless,
old as the earth.
            Insects came
to regard us with favor. I felt them alight,
felt their minute footfalls.
I was a challenge, an Everest . . .

And you, whom I have heard breathe all night,
sigh through the water of sleep
with vestigial gills . . .

A pair of dragonflies drifted past us, silent,
while higher up two bullet-shaped jets
dragged their roars behind them
on unbreakable chains. It seemed a pity
we'd given up the sky to them, but I understand so little.
Perhaps it was necessary.

All our years together—
and not just together. Surely by now
we have the same blood type, the same myopia.
Sometimes I think we're the same sex,
the one in the middle of man and woman,
born of both as every child is.

The waves came to us, one each heartbeat,
and lay themselves at our feet.
The swelling goes down.
The fever cools.
There, where the Hartleys grew lettuce eighty years ago
bear and beaver, fox and partridge
den and nest and hunt
and are hunted. I wish I had the means
to give all the north back to itself, to let the pines
rise in the hayfield and the lilacs go wild.
But then where would we live?

I wanted that hour with you all winter—
I thought of it while I worked,
before I slept and when I woke,
a time when the tangled would straighten,
when contrition would become benediction:
the positive hour, shining like mica.
At last the wind brought it to us across the pond,
then took it up again, every last minute.

.   .   .   .

HEID E. ERDRICH
(1963–)

A member of the Turtle Mountain Band of Ojibwe, Heid E. Erdrich was raised in Wahpeton, North Dakota, where her parents taught at the Bureau of Indian Affairs boarding school. She was educated at Dartmouth College and Johns Hopkins University. The recipient of awards from The Loft Literary Center, Minnesota State Arts Board, Wordcraft Circle of Native Writers, and the Archibald Bush Foundation, she is the author of Fishing for Myth, The Mother's Tongue, *and coeditor of* Sister Nations: Native American Women Writers on Community. *She is cofounder, with her sister Louise Erdrich, of Birchbark Books Press and has taught at the University of St. Thomas.*

What Pregnant is Like

You get bigger.
I mean you enlarge,
diffuse, push boundaries,
cover the whole of woman,
man, and child. You balloon,
stretch in unexpected directions,
expand to contain whole lives with your
lone body. Your body becomes an extension,
a shelter built of love that takes the man in again
and again to hold all three inside. Such a good place,
such a good planet, so heavy you make your own gravity.

Offering: Words

Gichimookomaanimo: speaks American, speaks the Long Knives' language

Mother, if you look it up, is *source*,
(fount and fountainhead—origin,
provenance and provenience,
root) and *wellspring*.
Near her in the dictionary you will find
we all spring *mother-naked*,
(bare, stripped, unclothed, undressed, and raw)
with nothing but *mother-wit*
(brains, brain-power, sense) our *native wit*
with which we someday might *mother*,
(nurse, care for, serve, and wait on)
if we don't first look it up and discover
the fullness of its meaning.

Such interesting language, this *tongue*,
(our diction, idiom, speech, and vernacular)
also *sign language*,
(gesture language)
and *contact language*,

which was English or Ojibwe,
either way; both spoke forward our *mother country*,
our *motherland* (see also fatherland,
our home, our homeland, our land)
called *soil* in English our *mother tongue*,
our *native language* that is not my *Native language*
not the *mother language* Ojibwe:
wellspring of many tongues, nurse, origin, and source.

Poem for Our Ojibwe Names

Those stars shine words right
into the center of the dream.

Gego zegizi kane.
Gego zegizi kane.
Maaji'am
Maaji nii'm
Maaji gigidoon.

So it is when we have our names.

We will not fear.
We start to sing,
to dance, to speak.

When we did not know him
the stick man, the running man,
came jigging in our dreams.
Always in motion like a wooden toy,
he sang "*Bakenatay, Bakenatay*"
so deeply his voice was a root.

So too the woman wrapped in red wool,
whose laughter woke us, "*Chi Wabeno.*"
She spoke the word for dreamers—

then teased in diminishment, "*Waban-ish.*"
Still her meaning took us years to learn.

Gego zegizi kane.
Gego zegizi kane.
Maajii'am
Maajii nii'm
Maajii gigidoon.

So it is when we have our names:
We will not fear.
We start to sing,
to dance, to speak.

It is not what you imagine,
no matter what you imagine.
Stars shine stories.
Words come speaking into our dreams.

.   .   .   .

DENISE SWEET
(1952–)

"I remember the old people speaking fervently to me about the real old sto-
ries," writes Denise Sweet, "about the importance of keeping the language
alive." Born on the Ojibwe reservation at White Earth, Sweet was educated
at the University of Wisconsin—Eau Claire and serves as professor of hu-
manistic studies at the University of Wisconsin—Green Bay. The recipient
of many awards for her work, she is the author of five collections of poetry,
including Know My Heart *and* Songs for Discharming, *winner of*
the Diane Decorah Award from the Native Writers' Circle of the Ameri-
cas. In 2004, she was named Poet Laureate of Wisconsin.

Constellations

. . . They had to name, they had to remember, or things would not
be named and remembered if they did not do it.
Carlos Fuentes

These are the new stories,
our response
to the sorrow
of light arriving
and dying
the stellar maps of
story and myth
where writers find
their way back
to beginnings
riding like black
satin horses
charging the silvery landscape.

This is to remember

Our wounded and
dead. This is to remember
the names
we've given away
or never received.
This is to love the forgotten.

Dancing the Rice

The fall season enters the rhythms of our pace
leaves gather like whorls on a spindle of wind
twisting and coiling around our feet;

the old man sits in front of the fire stirring
and singing low in whispers to himself, tossing
the rice slowly in the bottom of the black pot;

the good grain, manomin, turns slowly from green
to darkened fibers in the heat, we watch it turn
small swirls of steam wisp away from the parching;

the helper, a young man, slowly slips into moccasins
recalls that they belonged to his grandmother, and once
were too small for his feet—but they grew with him;

when we dance, he says, we caress the earth
we carry power in the way we present ourselves
as dancers, as singers, bringing the rice home;

this power enters each stem of manomin
but it must be a gentle step, the padding of feet
against the good grain; they hold our dreams

and we must be slow and gentle when we dance the rice
or they can quickly turn to broken stems and then to dust
then we have nothing and the manomin will not return.

He lowers himself into the barrel of parched rice
placing his feet gently against the heated grain
slowly lifting one foot, and twisting the other

he shifts his hips side to side; hoisting his weight
on the sides of the barrel, he gently kneads the grain
pressing each step in a circle against the barrel's bottom

"Everything tries to go in a circle. Everything in nature.
  You and me. Yuh." The old man watches while the rice is
      tossed
from the basket into the air—tiny whirlwinds of chaff spring

forth like dervishes released from a magic lamp. The wind
sails them away from the winnowed rice—the grain chinks
   against
the birchbark basket in cadence with the dropping wrists and

the young man's swaying black hair—it is a dance of sweet
   and
gentle love—warming hearts and pleasing the old man who
   watches
and sees in circles, our survival embodied in the winds of
   October.

. . . .

RAY GONZALEZ
(1952–)

Ray Gonzalez was born in El Paso, Texas, and educated at Southwest Texas State University. He is the author of eight books of poetry, including The Heat of Arrivals *(recipient of the Josephine Miles Book Award),* Cabato Sentora, The Hawk Temple at Tierra Grande, *and* Consideration of the Guitar: New and Selected Poems. *He has also authored two books of fiction and three volumes of nonfiction, and edited twelve anthologies. His many awards include a 1993 Before Columbus American Book Award for Excellence in Editing, a 1998 Colorado Governor's Award for Excellence in the Arts, and two Minnesota Book Awards. He teaches in the creative writing program at the University of Minnesota.*

Emerge

As if the sacred is the only way
and desire is fortune spilled across the desert
where no one has stepped in years.

As if the fever lifted from rage could change
the world and stir the holy water
tinged with blood.

As if the fallen song was a great mystery
and its rhyme came from the unfed mouths
of those who promised they would not weep.

As if the willow tree was a warning of green
and falling things resisting the broken ground.

As if listing the very heart of truth was outlawed
by a summer afternoon impossible to breathe.

As if each thing accomplished was taken away
by those who don't speak, but rearrange
the candles to ward off the starving spirit.

As if music in the fingers was played in time
to hear the heron rise, its flapping wings
changing the river into a pond.

As if a thousand rocks left one stone to emerge
through the decaying monument where no
one said anything as the mountain arrived.

As if the one thing we believe was finally
played on a guitar carved from the wood
of our father's crib.

As if the darkness is the beloved teacher
and its tool the mightiest reason
to go there together, unafraid.

As if the sacred is the only way
and the difficulties are lined up on the shelf
decorating the hallway into the interior.

where the names we are called
are the names of those who emerge.

What You Will Remember

The blue stone in the palm of the hand.
The orange held between the breasts.
A hawk dead in the middle of the road.
The dry tree bursting through the adobe.

The half-burned church in Chamberino
blackened and open to the sky.
A field of cotton with two men running across.
The saint in the window.

The road to Cochiti and the pass
to the last desert town.
The red stone from the agate beach,
hundreds of seabirds disappearing
beyond the island of fog.

No one in the window.
The smell of chorizo frying in the air,
sound of a lone gunshot across the night.
The dog dead in the middle of the road.

The eagle flying above the car
outside the ruins at Abo.
A green stone worn around the neck
as the mango is sliced to be eaten.

The river drying, reappearing within hours.
An old woman carrying a broken wooden chair,
a hedge of enormous cactus blocking her house,
green and white streamers blowing on telephone poles.

The barbed wire surrounding the church.
A huge lizard on the fence at the rest stop.
The closed eyes of La Virgin.
A man mistaken for a ghost crossing the road.

The headlights of a distant tractor.
Hands rubbing a headstone again and again.
The lacquered shoes on the bookshelf from
a tiny baby who never made it.

Celebrate

I am going to carry my river to the end
of the earth and celebrate.
I am going to wear my hat, then
whisper to the mice under the floor,
not hesitate in asking the stars to quit
burning so I can teach myself my
own prayers for a change.

When the car comes for me,
I will get in and be taken away.
The road will be full of birds,
sparrows and cardinals that flew
away from me long ago.
When I reach the moon,
my father will already be there,
wearing his own hat.
He will send me back on
the same river, my beard longer
than the white hair on the head
of the angriest god.

I will set foot on the driest land, wait
for the trees to grow and teach me
how to live under their shade.
I am going to love the places

where I have never been,
emerge from under those trees
in time to greet the stranger
who says to me, "Late. Late.
You are very late."

.　.　.　.

G. E. PATTERSON
(n. d.)

Poet, translator, and art critic, G. E. Patterson was educated at Stanford and Princeton universities and has been awarded fellowships from the Minnesota State Arts Board, the Jerome Foundation, and the University of Minnesota. The author of To and From *and* Tug *and recipient of the 2003 Minnesota Book Award, he has taught at Saint Mary's College of California and Metropolitan State University in St. Paul.*

Remembrance

My parents, being race people, taught me
by example: stand tall, speak up & look
straight in a man's eyes; there is real honor
in keeping the back of your head well-combed,
in old shoes you've polished to a hard shine,
in knowing your history and not telling your business.
My parents, being race people, saw that
things Black were put forward—pushing me on
to copy out the lives of Black heroes:
Benjamin Banneker, Ida B. Wells,
James Forton and Charlotte Forton, John Jasper,
Fannie Lou Hamer, Mary Church Terrell;
Marian Anderson, Henry O. Flipper,
Roy Wilkins, W. E. B. Du Bois;
Jackie Robinson, John C. Robinson,
Paul Robeson, Mary McLeod Bethune;
Major Taylor, Matthew Henson, Ralph Bunche.

My parents, being race people, knew things,
in this world, would be changed only by work. Hard work,
they told and told me, was the rock of faith.
Hard work, the whipstitch that kept cloth from fraying.

My parents, being race people, believed that
whatever I needed to know I'd learn
best from those who looked like, and looked out for, me.
There was no good reason to go outside
the neighborhood. Our one hope for salvation—
as a race, as a people—was ourselves.
Men and women fighting for more respect
lived up and down the block in well-kept homes
and low-rent apartments near the new Center
for Black Power. They worked long days and nights
at jobs I knew almost nothing about,
except their lawfulness. They were Black
in every imaginable way—yellow,
brown, redbone, blue-black (which we called inky),
oatmeal—colors lumped together like light,
a spectrum of miscegenation, broken
and united by love, like a family.

My parents, being race people, told me,
Everything good in them is good and Black,
I would do well if I learned to be like them,
I would do well to call them *Sir* and *Ma'am.*

Autobiography of a Black Man

> *Who has not*
> *On occasion entertained the presence*
> *Of a blackman?*
> Raymond Patterson

All the ladies feeling lucky at love
ask me if I like jazz, want to go out

and kick it at some club they know. I nod,
being a man who never disappoints.
Every white man I've known has wanted me
to join his basketball team, softball league
or book-discussion group. They invite me
on week-long, fly-fishing trips to Montana.
One day I might say yes. They think
they admire my superb athletic skills
and my broad education, but it's nothing
more than my color. I am The Black Man
the whole world mythologizes and envies.
I can get cats to march like boot-camp soldiers.
No dog ever dares ignore what I say—
sit up, fetch, play dead—the whole fucking routine.
Even New York roaches know to behave,
scurrying and hiding when I say, *Scat!*
I'm big and too damn powerful. The boss
on the job gulps hard and fast while I piss
into the cracked urinal. His hand shakes
as he follows me out, making small talk.
I will appear in his dreams 'til he's dead.
Black brothers, too, hurt themselves to get near me,
like crabs trying to climb out of a bucket.
The Latinos up in Harlem yell, *Jesus!*
when they see me. They fall down on their knees.
Am I the Messiah? Might be. Might be.
Koreans behind fruit stands bow their heads,
treating me like Buddha. That's alright. Let 'em.
My father wants us to be better friends
as if father and son weren't close enough.
My mother loves me more now than before,
since I grew up and became a Black man.
I'm twenty-three, and I'm king of this world.
Everyone fears and worships me. I know
I'm the motherfucking object of envy.
I'm the be-all and end-all of this world.

. . . .

ANGELA SHANNON
(1964–)

Born in Tulsa, Oklahoma, Angela Shannon holds a Master of Fine Arts degree from Warren Wilson College. Awards for her work include an Illinois Arts Council Fellowship in Poetry, the Willow Review Prize in Poetry, and a Career Initiative Grant from the Loft Literary Center. The author of Singing the Bones Together, *she lives in Minneapolis and has taught at the Loft, North Hennepin Community College, and Minneapolis Community and Technical College.*

Sunday

It could have been the way the Southern man
in his navy suit and skin rocked
along the church wall, swaying to the tambourine
like an old man wobbling to blues.

Or the way Sister Nettie got the spirit
all in her feet and behind, quick-stepping
like an ant hill was under her toes,
shaking her head back and forth in disbelief—

Or the way Deacon Jones raised
both hands like the police were there,
and started pacing the pulpit—
a foreign street—looking for Jesus.

But something quick came over the church
when Walter's voice slid to his navel
and plucked a piece of umbilical cord,
tugging the notes from generations gone.

And a sister lost in the crowd screamed,
like when children have their first babies,
and screeching floated over the pews
and took the congregation rocking

back to the first cry we made
in this freedom-stealing country—
the first shout on the auction block,
and we tried to clap our way out of memory,

to stomp out the sound like sparks of fire
but it was already voice (and the seer had said,
this child would be different).

Carrying Home

I am carrying home in my breast pocket:
land where I learned to crawl,
dust that held my footprints,
long fields I trod through.

Home, where Mother baked bread,
where Papa spoke with skies,
where family voices gathered.
In my palm, this heap of earth
I have hauled over hills and valleys.

Releasing dirt between my fingers,
I ask the prairies to sustain me.
May my soil and this soil nurture each other,
may seeds root and develop beyond measure,
may the heartland and I blossom.

.   .   .   .

KATRINA VANDENBERG
(1971–)

Katrina Vandenberg was raised in the Downriver area of Detroit, Michigan, and educated at Bowling Green University and the University of Arkansas. The recipient of a J. William Fulbright Fellowship to the Netherlands, a Bush Foundation Artist Fellowship, and a McKnight Foundation Fellowship in Poetry, she has served as visiting writer-in-residence at the Minneapolis College of Art and Design and the University of Arkansas. A resident of St. Paul, she is the author of one collection of poetry, Atlas.

First Lesson: The Anatomist Explains the Primacy of Imagination

These fontanelles of your skull won't close
for eighteen months; until then the bones remain
separate plates—frontal, parietal, occipital,
temporal, sphenoid—your concave spinal column
cannot hold. But instead of feeling helpless

when you sense the world outside yourself
and how little you can do, have faith in the world
of your head. Inside there, your skull bones work
to grow together, like the tectonic plates of the earth
in reverse, suturing and shaping as you evolve.

Your head, unlike the earth that sculpts mountains
to the sun, deepens dark grooves within
the brain's hemispheres to hold skeins
of butterflies inside, to show you oceans
and peninsulas without your even opening
your eyes. How different it will be there

from here, where pieces pulled apart until Africa
and Asia hoarded the elephants, and the penguins

clung to a single pole; where we harvest
the pods and seeds of the only spices we can grow,
then send them away in ships, with translators.

When your head is whole with fibrous joints
at the end of these eighteen months, think
how proud some cell in you somewhere will be,
of how its chemical impulse made again

a world with one country, a humming garden,
with the first vertebra, the atlas,
strong enough to hold it all upright.

Suppose

And what if you could step outside yourself,
could walk the streets of your old life after dark
until you found yourself in the lit window
of the bungalow on the April night you packed
your dead lover's clothes in a box you weighted
with his shoes, and saw yourself opening your arms

to fold his shirts? And then walked on. What if
we all could be this generous, cleaving ourselves
from the brief gasps of lilacs in our own yards,
from the outgrown rooms with their sticks of incense
dropping their thin threads of ash?
What if we were willing to turn the corner

to walk the street that holds the sum of lives,
the gallery of women taping shut
the boxes of the clothes of the dead, labeling them
with permanent marker? Oh, and if we did not try

to say we knew what was inside
their Glad bags, rustling secrets from the curb,

but spoke of those boxes and bags in such a way
that everyone who listened could open them and find

the shirts and shoes of their own dead brothers,
and discarded hearts, the whispers
of missing sisters across twin beds, old letters,
old dolls, the names for unnamed terrors,
the trinkets they'd forgot—what if you could
make everyone rich with the things they had lost?
Wouldn't you be that generous, if you knew how?

.   .   .   .

Janet Holmes
(1956–)

Born in Libertyville, Illinois, Janet Holmes holds degrees from Duke University and Warren Wilson College. She is the author of The Physicist at the Mall, The Green Tuxedo, Humanophone, *and* F2F. *Her honors include a Bush Foundation Fellowship, a Minnesota State Arts Board Fellowship, a Minnesota Book Award, and the Ernest Sandeen Prize in Poetry. While living in Minnesota from 1990 to 1999, she taught at Macalester College, the University of Minnesota, and the Loft Literary Center. She currently teaches in the Master of Fine Arts in Creative Writing program at Boise State University and directs Ahsahta Press.*

Birding

Some pursue quantity, a lifelist
personalized to the range and predilections
of a patient soul with binoculars angled up,
pencil ready, the mind's handy abacus
poised to click the next accumulation;

some seek particular birds
that return each year, old regulars
sentimental about their habits;
some just want the exotic,
the deep hues, rich excesses of rainbow
animate and winged and seldom seen.
But wild isn't always where you want it—
off the deck where the siskins fed all winter
framed by the kitchen's glass. You go
upwind of the heap of roadkill
at the highway department's utilitarian lot
where carcasses rot behind the dinosaur plows,
the graders out of season. New habitat.
What's struck by a truck goes back
to its role as provender, as surely
as if wolves patrolled these parts again:
whitetail gone to ribcage, their unaesthetic bones
marking the carnage where flyhatch
happens. Because of the semi
speeding down 61, you scope
warblers spangling the decomposing mound
with their brilliant golds,
the crimsons you covet.

The Blue World

There, says the guidebook, they live
in peace all winter: tunnels glowing glacier-blue

in the short afternoons, the worst predators
gone, gone, gone: it's frozen,

but under the snow a paradise
of shrews, thirteen-lined ground squirrels,

deer mice, voles, who feed for months
on the forest floor. There's no

wind. The air warms
in the narrow channels. Silence.

Silence. True, some scrabble
up to the crusted surface, discontent

with the crystal walls, the delicate
ice-carved rooms. True, the great grey owl

hears its prey through a three-foot snowfall:
slim weasels negotiate the maze:

dangers, even now. A vole
emerging into the winter trail

surprises a lapdog out for its walk,
whose dormant instincts quicken:

who seizes it. Shakes it dead.
Drop it, girl! Good girl! We pass

the fresh crater a squirrel made, having exited
a high branch—

and its quick prints off to a different
safety. So comic: a pratfall!

Here, my love: something to make you laugh.
No, no, I'm happy. Honestly. Light,

filtered and blue, softened, all afternoon
through the cold walls—

Really I am. See, I'm smiling.

.   .   .   .

LESLIE ADRIENNE MILLER
(1956–)

A resident of St. Paul, Leslie Adrienne Miller holds degrees from Stephens College, the University of Missouri, the University of Iowa, and the University of Houston. Awards for her work include the Loft-McKnight Poetry of Distinction Award, a National Endowment for the Arts Fellowship, the PEN Southwest Discovery Award, a Pushcart Prize, and the Anne Stanford Poetry Prize. Her books include Eat Quite Everything You See, Yesterday Had a Man in It, Ungodliness, *and* Staying Up Late For Love. *She teaches in the department of English at the University of St. Thomas in St. Paul.*

The Harriers

Memorial Day, 2004

Low over the swamp birch and sweet gale,
the broad torment of their shadows fall
on the marsh's invisible busy and small.
Snakes and shrews ride the roots, mice lurch
from one tussock to the next. The many
always fodder for the few, their tiny
pointed teeth useless in the sky.

Toothlessness lightens the harriers' skulls,
so they lift like foam, and belief wants to go
with them criss-crossing the marsh.
But the harriers, laying their hollow
bones on the wind, are only beautiful.
The male floats backward on the air
of his own arrival, passing his catch
to his mate in the sedge and gives me
one long look as he sits in the dead tree
at the edge of the marsh, curved, owlish head
cocked, funneling the small teedle-dee

of a distant rodent to its ear. *Harrier*
is from *harrow*, to torment, harass, assault,
also a cultivating implement set with spikes
for pulverizing soil. Significance falls apart
in my hands like a mist, though the harriers
have warm blood and four-chambered hearts.

The world they are offers no architecture
for an ethic: one dead language simply
rises through another, *raptor, rapture*,
and *rape*, for example, all sharing one
Latin root, *rapere, to seize*. The harriers
are only beautiful and will not be pressed

into resurrections. Even the highly significant
snake, hanging like a thread in the sky's white
neverending, knows the beetle in its belly isn't
his own and rides the talon of its captor,
who, when terror stands up and walks,
might be some kind of savior after all.

Mirabilia, 1726

The local doctor took her for a 'gloomy' sort,
a little daft, but strong. Her husband worked in cloth
and got on her three live young before this last,
most curious brood, a whole tribe of *Rabbets*
springing forth in groups of three or four.
Harvest in Godalming, Surrey, being nearly done,
and maybe that year only meager store,
leeks and turnips, a few thick-skinned gourds,
perhaps they'd been a little short, but rabbits
were abundant, and her boy able in getting
litters young and whole enough to plant
in Mary's lap, her roomy burrow readied
from easy passage of three prior infant

skulls. The village ready too for some miracle
of birth, even if it was just rabbits coming on
with winter's chill. By her own report, Mary took
a "longing" in the field one day, when a rabbit
sprang up like a bright idea from the dying
Queen Anne's lace and giant fennel,
so her five weeks' child afloat in the womb
fell away that night with a dream.
These blind and skinless babies curled
in the child's lost place and drank
of her waters, waited for light
and a man-midwife ready with belief.
Even after churching, more rabbits fell
from her marvelous loins in Guildford,
so the English Court brought her into town
to have a look, and though they caught
the serving boy with pockets full of blind
and slippery bunnies and trundled Mary Tofts
off to jail after her confession, the fact
remained that she had fooled at least
a half a dozen educated men by simply
being what she was, mammal, mystery,
cave and warren, unmapped womb,
a woman.

Madame du Coudray's Woman Machine, 1756

I perfected an invention that pity made me imagine.
Madame Le Boursier du Coudray, *Abrégé*

After D'Agoty's macabre écorchés
and Rymsdyck's tendency to coil
his innards tight as bags of fists
and then to paint a fatty sheen
on every part, I gasp out loud
when I find Le Boursier's soft machine

of linen and leather, the woman's thighs
great hams of rosy fabric gathered
at the knees like parlor bolsters,
the plush swell of belly draped
in a modest apron opened in a V,
that all who would deliver her
might see the fine embroidery
of the wrinkled vulva giving way
to the crowning cloth doll, one puffed
umbilical cord to announce life,
another flat to advertise a death.
While D'Agoty's sexy écorchés
live on in countless volumes, only one
of Madame du Coudray's *machines*
for instruction in the art of birth
remains, this one with its wicker bones
and wooden pelvis replaces her original
which tucked a gate of real pelvic bones
inside the giant cushion. Sundry detached
pieces lie about: the pillowy placenta
as if infused with waters still, the warning
of a crushed and severed infant skull
to show the damage of an unforgiving tug.
She made her mannequin of cloth
for the women of Clermont who couldn't read,
much less afford D'Agoty's illustrated books,
who worried more about the warming
of the wine and butter in which a living child
was cleansed, or the sturdy shoes the dead
would need for traveling hard dark roads
to nurse their babies from the grave.
She listened while they spoke of prolapse,
mangled parts, torn limbs and broken backs,
the ragged, filthy fingernail of someone's
helpful aunt or neighbor tearing the sight
from a child's eye. From these tales
she fashioned her machine, pushing

her needles through the flesh colored cloth
as capably as she pushed her hands,
merciful and clean, into the darkened rooms
of a thousand unupholstered wombs.

.   .   .   .

WANG PING
(1957–)

Wang Ping was born in Shanghai and educated at Beijing University, Long Island University, and New York University. She is the author of the novel Foreign Devil *and the short story collections* American Visa *and* The Last Communist Virgin, *and the editor and co-translator of* New Generation: Poetry from China Today. *Her poetry collections include* Of Flesh & Spirit *and* The Magic Whip. *The recipient of fellowships from the National Endowment for the Arts, the New York Foundation for the Arts, the Minnesota State Arts Board, and the Bush Foundation, she lives in St. Paul and teaches at Macalester College.*

I Curse Because

You say the streets are paved with gold.
You say even the maids have maids.
If we work hard, our dreams will be fulfilled.
So we come—on foot,
by boats, ships, planes.

"Do me a favor, and get a new name," said my boss. "Something American, like us."

In the alleys and backstreets of Chinatown are job agencies, where opium dens and brothels used to be. We gather

behind the barred windows and iron gates, waiting to be
dispatched as cooks, dishwashers, delivery boys, as
receptionists, waitresses, nannies, housekeepers, button
sewers. We work under the table for minimum wage.

First bite of pizza—throw up on the boss's shoes.
Dirty streets littered with the homeless.
No public toilets on American streets.
Can't understand a word, despite my English degree
   from Beijing University.
Armani suit man spits on the sidewalk.
Pork tastes like woodchips, tomatoes like mud.
Lost in the subway maze.
So high the skyscrapers, so low my basement.
Vast shopping malls, my empty wallet.

"Please, please become an American citizen,"
my brother begged me over the phone,
his voice severed by the long-distance wire.
"This is   the only   way   I can   come   to   America."

To keep my job, I changed my name to Penelope, then
Penny. For ten years, I was known as Penny Wan.

Through the barred windows of Ellis Island, we gazed at
Manhattan's silhouette. Paradise was only a river away.
Around us were the names of the deportees—the sick, low
wits, anarchists, criminals, potential prostitutes—names
carved into the walls with pens, brushes, nails, knives.

This is how you bus a table, as she stacked dirty plates on
   her arm.
This is how you serve clients, she grinned, her face a mask
   of meekness and rage.
If they spit in your face, turn the other cheek.
If they forget to leave a tip, smile and say "Welcome
   back."

Forget about your Ph.D., having taught in Beijing
    University.
You start from here, zero, she stamped the ground, hard.

We know the stink and hunger of a ship's hold. We know
the unforgiveness of the desert. We may be raped, drowned,
dehydrated, caught, deported. May never pay off the loans
to the snakeheads. May end up dead in a sealed truck, in the
sea, become ghosts in deserts and foreign streets. We know.
We know it all. From rumors, stories, eyewitnesses, movies.
But we're still coming, like marching ants, locusts, tidal
waves. The moon guides us, pulling us to the other shore, by
the heart.

The boy knelt into the sand, and kissed the soil of America.

Eight moves within eight months: Flushing, Brooklyn,
Elmhurst, Harlem, Elmhurst, Rego Park, Flushing,
Flushing. Finally a steady income from a law office—$5 an
hour cash, and moved into a house on Farrington Street,
Flushing. $200 a month, heat and electricity. Across the
street, a Korean brothel. Sharing kitchen and bathroom
with a Vietnamese, a Malaysian, two Fu Jian ship jumpers.
Our Hong Kong landlady believed in energy saving. Two
hours of heat a day—more than enough. Taped our windows
with plastic, wore sweaters, coats, hats, and gloves to bed.
Fought over the toilet and stove, over who ate what in the
refrigerator. But we held out. This was our home. Our
dream.

Restaurants and gift shops line Chinatown streets like
    crows.
I constantly got lost in the maze, even though the Twin
    Towers
stood a few blocks away.

The U.S. consulate rejected my brother's third application. He talked about borrowing thirty thousand dollars from snake-heads and jumping ship.

> Did you have a toilet? bath? hot water?
> Could you afford a car? a house? three children?
> Color TV? VCR? Laptop?
> Could you say whatever you wanted in your own country?

Last stop Flushing. Run up the subway steps. Do not look around. Do not glance at the car purring along Farrington Street. Do not panic at his open fly, pale hand up and down under the wheel, ring gleaming in the moonlight. Do not hear the whispered beckoning: Hey pigtailed China doll, won't you come with me?

"You're in America now, you have nothing to fear," said my sponsor at JFK.

He inches his van through fish and vegetable stands, through underwear, bras, slippers, perfumes, through baseball hats, dragon T-shirts, Chanel bags, through throngs of shoppers and gawking tourists. "Too many Chinese, too many fucking Chinese!" he mutters as he enters the heart of Chinatown.

"Don't tell me it's impossible. I'm willing to wait five, ten years. I'm willing to work, restaurants, laundromats. I just want my daughter to have a good education and freedom to choose where she wants to live, like you, Sister."

5:00 A.M. The old man arrives at Confucius Plaza. Feet apart. Knees bent. Hands before the chest. A ball of fire. Sixty years of tai chi. Under the statue. Never missed a day. Since the ship's arrival. No wife. No children to inherit his savings. He's an American, an overseas Chinese, venerable Laundromat Wong on East Broadway.

We've been deloused, tagged, marked with chalk.
We've answered questions like "How many legs does a
      horse have?"
We've been stripped, poked in the eyes, ears, private parts.
When the officer called our names aloud,
we ran down the steps, screaming,
into the arms of our estranged fathers, husbands,
      brothers, and sisters.

Go to Ellis Island. Go find your ancestor on the Wall of
Honor. Trace it. Trace with a pencil. On paper. Our
ancestors. 500,000 names. More to come. Inscribed.
Steeled.

I sent home $400, my first month's earnings as a waitress,
along with a photo of myself at the airport, grinning from
behind a trunk, two fingers heavenward in the shape of a v.

What do you really want?
What more do you want?

Mixed Blood

At fifteen, my father ran away from his widowed mother to
fight the Japanese.

"I'll come back with a Ph.D. and serve my country with
better English and knowledge," I pledged at the farewell
party in Beijing.

Home — 家 — *jia:* a roof under which animals live.

When asked where I'm from,
I say "Weihai," even though
nobody knows where it is,
even though I've never been to that place.

He lost his left ear in a bayonet fight with a Japanese soldier.
Two years later, American cannons split his eardrums.

The night I arrived at JFK, the Mets won the World Series
and the noise on the street went on till three. I got up at
six and went to work in my sponsor's antique shop in
Manhattan.

The bag lady stopped her cart on the busy street and peed
onto a subway grate.

"Did you jump or fly?" asked my landlady from her mah-
jongg table. Then she laughed and told me that her husband
had jumped ship ten years ago. When he opened his fifth
Chinese take-out, he bought her a passport and flew her to
Queens.

The only thing he liked to talk about was his old home, Wei-
hai, its plump sea cucumbers and sweet apples, men with
broad shoulders, stubborn thighs, and girls with long braids
making steamed bread.

"I don't know why," she said, shivering behind her fruit stand.
"Back home, I could go for days without a penny in my
pocket, and I didn't feel poor. Now, if my money goes down
below four figures, I panic." She scanned the snow-covered
streets of Chinatown. "I guess I really don't want to be
homeless here."

I hired the babysitter when she mentioned that her
hometown was Weihai.

The president visited the rice paddies in Vietnam where a
pilot had been downed thirty-three years ago.

My father tried to return to Weihai after his discharge from
the Navy. With his rank, he could find work only in a

coalmining town nearby. My mother refused to go. He went alone, and soon contracted TB. Mother ordered me to date the county administrator's son so my father could come home.

"No, I'm not sad." The street kid shook her head.
"How can I miss something I've never had?"

On her sixtieth birthday, my grandma went home to die. She would take two ships, one from the island to Shanghai, then from Shanghai to Yantai. From there, she would take two buses to reach Weihai. I carried her onto the big ship at the Shanghai Port, down to the bottom, where she'd spend three days on a mattress, on the floor, with hundreds of fellow passengers. "How are you going to make it, Grandma?" I asked. She pulled out a pair of embroidered shoes from her parcel and placed them between my feet. "My sweetheart and liver, come to see your old home soon, before it's too late."

House— 房 —*fang*: a door over a square, a place, a direction.

He never lost his accent, never learned Mandarin or the island dialect.

Weihai, a small city
in Shandong Province,
on the coast of the North China Sea,
a home, where my grandfather
and his father were born,
where my grandma married,
raised her children, and
now lies in the yam fields,
nameless, next to her husband,
an old frontier to fend off Japanese pirates,
a place I come from, have never seen.

Back from America, my mother furnished her home on the
island, bought an apartment in a suburb of Shanghai, and is
considering a third one in Beijing. "A cunning rabbit needs
three holes," she wrote to her daughters, demanding their
contributions.

They swore, before boarding the ship, that they'd send
money home to bring more relatives over; in return, they
were promised that if they died, their bodies would be sent
back home for burial.

> I drink American milk—a few drops in tea.
> I eat American rice—Japanese brand.
> Chinese comes to me only in dreams—in black-and-
> white pictures.

My mother buried her husband on the island, where he
  lived for forty years.

Room— 屋 — *wu:* a body unnamed and homeless until it
  finds a destination.

> We greet a stranger with,
> "Where are you from?"
> When we meet a friend on the street, we say,
> "Where have you been? Where are you going?"

家— a roof under which animals live
房— a door over a square, a place, a direction
屋— a body unnamed and homeless until it finds a
  destination

                    —my tangled roots for home.

· · · ·

ED-BOK LEE
(n. d.)

Born in Fargo, Ed-Bok Lee was raised in North Dakota, South Korea, California, and Minnesota. Upon graduation from the University of Minnesota, he studied Slavic and Central Asian Languages and Literatures at Kazakh State University in Kazakhstan, Indiana University, and the University of California at Berkeley, eventually receiving a Master of Fine Arts degree from Brown University. The recipient of awards for his poetry, prose, and plays from the Jerome Foundation, Minnesota State Arts Board, and the National Endowment for the Arts, he is the author of Real Karaoke People: Poems and Prose.

Sokcho in Butterfly Dust

Beside my father's window hung a portrait
of Sokcho—a seaside village where lather laps
the morning shore like cold rice porridge.
A watercolor adorned with butterfly pluckings: tiny
fishermen on docks pulling rods of antennae,
silk lines cast beneath a flaming dusk
of fanned Harlequin wings.

I'd imagine the blithe figures
whistling to work in the fall.
Sadly-happy Korean faces, hung over
from soju, smoked squid, and cards till dawn.
Sometimes I'd enter the shadowy port;
rock asleep inside any one of the turquoise junks
as the moon's mothy swoosh brightened a path
back across the ocean.

Life should always be this easy to find.
A small boy waiting for his father to return for dinner.

Meanwhile, esoteric seafarers travel
back and forth between one rough, one finer world,

on land, over sea and the coral
trove we learn to navigate
by drowning.

The Invisible Church

A park in a country.
But which country?

If you ask the Somali men hovering
over ancient chessboard tables
and apple tea where they are,
they'll tell you a constant state of waiting.
And that all the broken glass on the sidewalk
reminds how dangerous it is to pray on their knees
in Arabic these days.

The Hmong man with military medals and a gray goatee
bears a different story. He plays it on his kher,
a two-string spidery bamboo violin he leans into,
slicing open one ghost at a time with his bow.
If he set out a hat, or tin can, maybe
all the shoes hating dead leaves
wouldn't sound so lonely.

A war and a Tuesday afternoon.

But which war? If you stop
the glaucomic Polish Jew who hobbles
past crackheads on picnic tables feeling their bones,
or young do-rags dreaming new tags,
that punctual spirit, he might tell you
he escaped from a concentration camp by hand-washing
    yellow stains
from SS pillow cases and bed sheets; propelled
to safety through a laundry chute and survived
the winter forest on roots and worms. . . .

Or, this autumn, he might just say the crude
tattoo numbered on the inside of his wrist
is a postage stamp on a strange envelope
lost in transit.

Actually, he's probably heading to the thrift store
to see if any stained-glass lamps, board games,
or good cutlery came in.

A country and a soul.

Among a hip hop boom box and Russian card game on a
     one-board bench;
an old drunk Mexicano in straw cowboy hat and white
     beard,
belting a cappella harvest hymns of a woman with bad
     intentions
and the scrawny mutt who pants in front of me,
leash in mouth . . .

There is a small city park and fountain
presided over by the Saint of Looted Expression.
Some days after work I'll breach the dry basin
and sit at the statue's bare feet. Read
a news page to assess the world's ever-fading progress.
I'll go until my eyes, the ink and evening
blend to a dangerous cocktail. Or
a jittery spirit approaches from nowhere
to ask in secret code for the church that burned down
long before either of us was born.

.   .   .   .

Mayli Vang
(1975–)

Mayli Vang was born in Xiengkhoang, Laos, and spent most of her childhood in southern California before moving with her family to Minnesota. A graduate of the College of St. Catherine, she works for a nonprofit health insurance company in St. Paul. Her writing has appeared in a number of journals and anthologies, including Paj Ntaub Voice, Bamboo Among the Oaks: Contemporary Writing by Hmong Americans, *and* Tilting the Continent: Southeast Asian Writing.

We Women of the Hmong Culture

We women of the Hmong culture
may now clean the plates
of what the men have left,
eat the remains while they pick
their teeth with wooden toothpicks.

They call this a privilege,
to be seated at the table
of those who were seated before.
To partake in this feast of remains

is a blessing beyond all measures.
Yet some she-witched women
"possessed by this newfound knowledge
of excessive freedom" are weary

of participating in such patriarchal
rituals of the old motherland.
They stare at the remains of half-eaten
meat—the imprints of a beloved uncle's

teeth still cut upon them—littered
among the cuisine grown cold

from hours of neglect.
Does no one wish to sit and taste?

The host and hostess invite
all us women to partake in the feast
of *laab*—ground beef,
half-cooked tendons—and chicken

boiled with withered herbs.
Biting our lips and our tongues,
we sit. With each bite into the feast
at hand, we remember

we are women.

.   .   .   .

MAI NENG MOUA
(1974–)

Poet and creative nonfiction writer, Mai Neng Moua was educated at St. Olaf College and the Hubert H. Humphrey Institute of Public Affairs at the University of Minnesota. Cofounder of Paj Ntaub Voice, *a Hmong literary arts journal, and editor of* Bamboo Among the Oaks: Contemporary Writing by Hmong Americans, *the first Hmong American anthology of contemporary writing, she serves as the public policy coordinator for the Institute for New Americans, a nonprofit organization located in Minneapolis, and teaches creative writing to Hmong youth at the Jane Addams School for Democracy. The recipient of a Bush Foundation Fellowship, she lives in St. Paul.*

My Mother Is a Coffee Table

My mother is in the living room
And the kitchen and the bathroom
My father has gone fishing

She is on all fours
One for her three young children
Two for the unpaid bills
Three for her broken English
Four for . . . help!

With her head, she holds up the house

Father Died Twenty-five Years Ago

Father died twenty-five years ago
Now mother farms a four-acre plot of land
With a tiller and a Hmong hoe
She prepares for war
Selling vegetables to white *Mekas*
In her little stall at the farmers' market
Something father would've helped her with

Father died twenty-five years ago
Now sister works two full-time jobs
To pay for the house she bought for the family
So mother would not worry
This was something father would've done

Father died twenty-five years ago
Now older brother has to be the man of the house
Struggling to finish college
He has postponed marriage and children
Mother does not trust him
She says father was a colonel at brother's age

Father died twenty-five years ago
Now younger brother has gone off to war
Leaving behind his family
As father did twenty-five years ago
Mother says he is not like father

Father died twenty-five years ago

D.C.

I stood my ground
It's not enough that I am here
I want the imprints of their names
Some American proof that they were known
Their courage recognized
The sacrifices of their lives acknowledged
The ranger in khaki shorts and Smokey-the-Bear hat said
"You have to know someone who died there"
I stood my ground
Letting the emotions clog my throat, sting my eyes

What had I expected him to say
"Your father Tooj Cib Muas is right over here?"
My mute tongue could not scream
"But I do know someone who died there"
I know six who died there
Grandfather Soob Tseej Vws
Uncle Txooj Kuam Vws
Uncle Kim Vws
Uncle Looj Muas
Men who are supposed to be—
But are not—
Here taking care of me
Showing my little brother how to be a man

The white man had moved on
To other people—tourists gathered
Around the memorial as if
It was an exotic exhibit
Talking loudly, laughing, downing
Their Evian in the humid heat
Disturbing the memories of chaos
Just another thing you do while you're in D.C.

I stood my ground

. . . .

SPENCER REECE
(1963–)

Spencer Reece was born in Hartford, Connecticut, raised in Minneapolis and Edina, and educated at Bowdoin College, Wesleyan University, University of York, and the Harvard Divinity School. The author of The Clerk's Tale, *he is the recipient of numerous honors and awards for his work, including the Katharine Bakeless Mason Prize in Poetry and fellowships from the National Endowment for the Arts, the Guggenheim Foundation, the Witter Bynner Foundation, and the Whiting Foundation. After living for many years on his family's farm outside of Northfield, he moved to Juno Beach, Florida, where he now resides.*

The Clerk's Tale

I am thirty-three and working in an expensive clothier,
selling suits to men I call "Sir."
These men are muscled, groomed and cropped—
with wives and families that grow exponentially.
Mostly I talk of rep ties and bow ties,
of full-Windsor knots and half-Windsor knots,

of tattersall, French cuff, and English spread collars,
of foulards, neats, and internationals,
of pincord, houndstooth, nailhead, and sharkskin.
I often wear a blue pin-striped suit.
My hair recedes and is going gray at the temples.
On my cheeks there are a few pimples.
For my terrible eyesight, horn-rimmed spectacles.
One of my fellow-workers is an old homosexual
who works hard and wears bracelets with jewels.
No one can rival his commission checks.
On his break he smokes a Benson & Hedges cigarette,
puffing expectantly as a Hollywood starlet.
He has carefully applied a layer of Clinique bronzer
to enhance the tan on his face and neck.
His hair is gone except for a few strands
which are combed across his scalp.
He examines his manicured lacquered nails.
I admire his studied attention to details:
his tie stuck to his shirt with masking tape,
his teeth capped, his breath mint in place.
The old homosexual and I laugh in the back
over a coarse joke involving an octopus.
Our banter is staccato, staged and close
like those "Spanish Dances" by Granados.
I sometimes feel we are in a musical—
gossiping backstage between our numbers.
He drags deeply on his cigarette.
Most of his life is over.
Often he refers to himself as "an old faggot."
He does this bemusedly, yet timidly.
I know why he does this.
He does this because his acceptance is finally complete—
and complete acceptance is always
bittersweet. Our hours are long. Our backs bent.
We are more gracious than English royalty.
We dart amongst the aisles tall as hedgerows.
Watch us face into the merchandise.

How we set up and take apart mannequins
as if we were performing autopsies.
A naked body, without pretense, is of no use.
It grows late.
I hear the front metal gate close down.
We begin folding the ties correctly according to color.
The shirts—Oxfords, broadcloths, pinpoints—
must be sized, stacked, or rehashed.
The old homosexual removes his right shoe,
allowing his gigantic bunion to swell.
There is the sound of cash being counted—
coins clinking, bills swishing, numbers whispered—
One, two, three, four, five, six, seven . . .
We are changed when the transactions are done—
older, dirtier, dwarfed.
A few late customers gawk in at us.
We say nothing. Our silence will not be breached.
The lights go off, one by one—
the dressing room lights, the mirror lights.
Then it is very late. How late? Eleven?
We move to the gate. It goes up.
The gate's grating checkers our cheeks.
This is the Mall of America.
The light is bright and artificial,
yet not dissimilar to that found in a Gothic cathedral.
You must travel down the long hallways to the exits
before you encounter natural light.
One final formality: the manager checks our bags.
The old homosexual reaches into his over-the-shoulder
    leather bag—
the one he bought on his European travels
with his companion of many years.
He finds a stick of lip balm and applies it to his lips
liberally, as if shellacking them.
Then he inserts one last breath mint
and offers one to me. The gesture is fraternal
and occurs between us many times.

At last, we bid each other good night.
I watch him fade into the many-tiered parking lot,
where the thousands of cars have come
and are now gone. This is how our day ends.
This is how our day always ends.
Sometimes snow falls like rice.
See us take to our dimly lit exits,
disappearing into the cities of Minneapolis and St. Paul;
Minneapolis is sleek and St. Paul,
named after the man who had to be shown,
is smaller, older, and somewhat withdrawn.
Behind us, the moon pauses over the vast egg-like dome of
    the mall.
See us loosening our ties among you.
We are alone.
There is no longer any need to express ourselves.

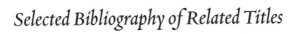

Selected Bibliography of Related Titles

Arnold, Mrs. W. J., ed. *The Poets and Poetry of Minnesota*. Chicago: S. P. Rounds, 1864.

Breen, Genevieve Rose, and Carmen Nelson Richards, eds. *Minnesota Writes*. Minneapolis: The Lund Press, 1945.

DeGrazia, Emilio and Monica, eds. *33 Minnesota Poets*. Minneapolis: Nodin Press, 2000.

Densmore, Frances. *Chippewa Music*. Bulletin 45, Bureau of American Ethnology, Smithsonian Institution, Washington, D.C., 1910.

———. *Chippewa Music II*. Bulletin 53, Bureau of American Ethnology. Smithsonian Institution, Washington, D.C., 1913.

———. *Poems from Sioux and Chippewa Songs*. Washington, D.C.: Smithsonian Institution, 1917.

Flanagan, John T. *Minnesota's Literary Visitors*. Minneapolis: Pogo Press, 1993.

Hanson, Felicity. *Minnesota Settler Poetry, 1840–1890: A Literary, Cultural, and Historical Study*. Honors thesis, Hamline University, 1999.

Joyce, Darlene Cruikshank. *Naming a Writing Community: Contemporary Authors in Minnesota*. Master's thesis, Hamline University, 1992.

Moore, Jim, and Cary Waterman, eds. *Minnesota Writes: Poetry*. Minneapolis: Milkweed Editions/Nodin Press, 1987.

Morrison, Julia Maria. *Literary Journals in Minnesota: November 1850–April 1961*. Master's thesis, University of Minnesota, 1961.

Moua, Mai Neng, ed. *Bamboo Among the Oaks: Contemporary Writing by Hmong Americans*. St. Paul: Minnesota Historical Society Press, 2002.

Northrup, Jim, et al. *Nitaawichige: Selected Poetry and Prose by Four Anishinaabe Writers*. Duluth, Minnesota: Poetry Harbor Press, 2002.

Nute, Grace Lee. *A History of Minnesota Books and Authors*. Minneapolis: University of Minnesota Press, 1958.

Richards, Carmen Nelson, ed. *Minnesota Writers*. Minneapolis: T. S. Denison & Co., 1961.

———. *Minnesota Skyline: Anthology of Poems About Minnesota*. Minneapolis: League of Minnesota Poets, 1944.

Riggs, Stephen Return. *Tah-koo Wah-kan; or the Gospel Among the Dakotas*. Boston: Congregational Publishing Society, 1869.

Schilpin, Maude C., ed. *Minnesota Verse: An Anthology*. St. Cloud, Minnesota: The Times Publishing Co., 1934 and 1938 (revised edition).

Schoolcraft, Henry Rowe. *Historical and Statistical Information Respecting the History, Condition, and Prospects of the Indian Tribes of the United States*. 6 vols. Philadelphia: Lippincott, Grambo, and Co., 1851–1857.

Sutphen, Joyce, Thom Tammaro, and Connie Wanek, eds. *To Sing Along the Way: Minnesota Women's Poetry from Territorial Days to the Present.* Moorhead, Minnesota: New Rivers Press, 2006.

Vale, Charles, ed. *The Spirit of St. Louis: One Hundred Poems.* New York: George H. Doran Co., 1927.

Vinz, Mark, ed. *Imagining Home: Writing from the Midwest.* Minneapolis: University of Minnesota Press, 1995.

Vinz, Mark, and Thom Tammaro, eds. *Inheriting the Land: Contemporary Voices from the Midwest.* Minneapolis: University of Minnesota Press, 1993.

Vizenor, Gerald, ed. *Summer in the Spring: Anishinaabe Lyric Poems and Stories.* Norman: University of Oklahoma Press, 1993.

Yesner, Seymour, ed. *25 Minnesota Poets.* Minneapolis: Nodin Press, 1974.

———. *25 Minnesota Poets #2.* Minneapolis: Nodin Press, 1978.

Permissions

Mai Neng Moua, published by Minnesota Historical Society Press, 2002. Reprinted by permission of the author.

"Red River Blues" and "Still Life with Thermometer" from *Red River Blues* by Mark Vinz. Copyright© 1977 by Mark Vinz. Reprinted by permission of the author. "Flat Country" from *Long Distance* by Mark Vinz, published by MWPH Books. Copyright© 2005 by Mark Vinz. Reprinted by permission of the author.

"After Us" and "Hartley Field" from *Hartley Field* by Connie Wanek. Copyright© 2002 by Connie Wanek. Reprinted by permission of the author and Holy Cow! Press.

"Crocus" from *When I Looked Back You Were Gone* by Cary Waterman. Copyright© 1992 by Cary Waterman. Reprinted by permission of the author and Holy Cow! Press. "Visiting the Mayo Clinic" from *The Salamander Migration* by Cary Waterman, published by University of Pittsburgh Press. Copyright© 1980 by Cary Waterman. Reprinted by permission of the author.

"An Ordinary Exposure" and excerpt from "Gatherings" from *The Salt Ecstasies* by James L. White. Copyright© 1982 by James L. White. Reprinted by permission of Graywolf Press, St. Paul, Minnesota.

"Dove" from *The Pomegranate Tree Speaks from the Dictator's Garden* by J. P. White, published by Holy Cow! Press. Copyright© 1988 by J. P. White. Reprinted by permission of the author and Holy Cow! Press. "Essay on Leaves" from *The Salt Hour* by J. P. White, published by University of Illinois Press. Copyright© 2001 by J. P. White. Reprinted by permission of the author.

"The Fall of the House of Usher," "The High School Band in September," and "When My Father Left in the Morning" from *The Past, The Future, The Present* by Reed Whittemore, published by University of Arkansas Press. Copyright© 1990 by Reed Whittemore. Reprinted by permission of the author.

"Tribute and Ash" from *Late Empire* by David Wojahn. Copyright © 1994 by David Wojahn. Reprinted by permission of the University of Pittsburgh Press. "Fort Snelling National Cemetery: St. Paul, Minnesota" (Part VII of the poem sequence titled "The Shades") from *The Falling Hour* by David Wojahn. Copyright© 1997 by David Wojahn. Reprinted by permission of the University of Pittsburgh Press.

"Lying in a Hammock at William Duffy's Farm in Pine Island, Minnesota," "A Blessing," and "The Minneapolis Poem" from *Collected Poems* by James Wright. Copyright© 1971 by James Wright. Reprinted by permission of Wesleyan University Press.

Index of Authors, Titles, and First Lines

Acknowledgments

I am indebted to several people who helped in the preparation of this book: Patrick K. Coleman, Heid E. Erdrich, Patricia Hampl, Benjamin Hedin, Carolyn Hedin, Timothy Johnson, Scott King, Sheila O'Connor, Jim Perlman, and Tammy Wadley. I am also grateful to the staff of the Red Wing Public Library for its help in researching the background of many of the poets. Above all, I wish to express my gratitude to those at the Minnesota Historical Society Press and Borealis Books—Gregory M. Britton, Ann Regan, and Pamela J. McClanahan —for their illuminations, professionalism, and unfailing commitment to make this collection possible. Thank you all.   RH

About the Editor

Born and raised in Red Wing, Minnesota, Robert Hedin holds degrees
from Luther College and the University of Alaska in Fairbanks. He is
the author, translator, and editor of nineteen volumes of poetry and
prose. Honors and awards for his work include three National Endow-
ment for the Arts Fellowships, two Minnesota Book Awards, a Bush
Foundation Fellowship, a McKnight Foundation Fellowship, a Min-
nesota State Arts Board Fellowship, a North Carolina State Arts
Council Fellowship, and the Loft Poetry of Distinction Award. In
1998, he was presented with the Arts Leadership Award by the Min-
nesota State Arts Board for his writing and contributions to the arts in
the state. He has taught at Sheldon Jackson College, the Anchorage
and Fairbanks campuses of the University of Alaska, St. Olaf College,
and Wake Forest University, where he served as poet-in-residence
from 1980 to 1992. In 2001–2002, he was named Edelstein-Keller
Minnesota Writer of Distinction at the University of Minnesota. He
is cofounder (with his wife, Carolyn) and current director of the An-
derson Center for Interdisciplinary Studies, an artist retreat, in Red
Wing, and coedits *Great River Review*.

Also by Robert Hedin

POETRY
The Old Liberators: New and Selected Poems and Translations
Tornadoes
County O
At the Home-Altar
Snow Country

TRANSLATIONS
A Bumpy Ride to the Slaughterhouse: Prose Poems of Dag T. Straumsvåg
    (with Louis Jenkins)
The Roads Have Come to an End Now: Selected and Last Poems of Rolf Jacobsen
    (with Robert Bly and Roger Greenwald)
The Bullfinch Rising from the Cherry Tree: Poems of Olav H. Hauge
The Dream Factory: A Children's Story by Bjørn Sortland
    (with Emily Christianson)
Night Music: Poems of Rolf Jacobsen
In Lands Where Light Has Another Color: Poems of Rolf Jacobsen

EDITED COLLECTIONS
Old Glory: American War Poems from the Revolutionary War to the War on Terrorism
Perfect in Their Art: Poems on Boxing from Homer to Ali (with Michael Waters)
Keys to the Interior: Twenty-five Years of the Great River Review
    (with Richard Broderick)
The Zeppelin Reader: Stories, Poems and Songs from the Age of Airships
The Great Machines: Poems and Songs of the American Railroad
The Great Land: Reflections on Alaska
    (with Gary Holthaus)
Alaska: Reflections on Land and Spirit
    (with Gary Holthaus)
In the Dreamlight: Twenty-one Alaskan Writers
    (with David Stark)

Where One Voice Ends Another Begins
was designed and set in type by Will Powers
at the Minnesota Historical Society Press
and was printed by Vail-Ballou Press, Binghamton, New York.

The typeface is Requiem, designed by Jonathan Hoefler.

Special thanks to Mike Kelsey at inari for the Chinese type.